The Child 'Protection Racket'

High-level Child Trafficking in Australia

DEE McLACHLAN

We understand there is an underground global market in child exploitation and sex trafficking (as represented in the movie, *Sound of Freedom*)

This book is about 'The Child Protection Racket' – the open and supposedly legalized system that trades and exploits children in Australia.

First edition (November 2023)

ISBN - 9798869940230

thechildprotectionracket.com

Note: The names of children and their parents have been changed to comply with the privacy laws; and identifying factors (or quotes) in any cases mentioned have been altered. (The foster parents' story had already been published in the media.)

Prologue

Ordinary Australians find it difficult to comprehend that children are being unwarrantedly and unlawfully removed from their loving parents. This book explains and documents how the State child protection system has become an apparatus to exploit and trade children for financial gain.

The culture of removing children from parents as a solution for keeping children safe is deeply entrenched in Australia. And for a parent to challenge a child department's decision is almost impossible; it's as if they have a 'no-return-policy'. Government agencies, medical professionals and judicial officers are ostensibly seduced into the 'crowd psychology' of 'removing' children where they act in unison, distancing themselves from compassion, rational forethought, and objectives of equity and law.

Australia is a signatory to the *International Covenant on Civil and Political Rights* (ICCPR) which recognizes the rights derived from inherent dignity, that "Everyone has the right to liberty and security of person… No one shall be deprived of his liberty" (Article 9),[1] and "All are equal before the law and are entitled without any discrimination to equal protection of the law" (Article 26).[2] Article 9 of the *United Nations Convention on the Rights of the Child* (UNCRC) ensures that "a child shall not be separated from his or her parents against their will…"

As you read through this book, you will decide for yourself whether human rights and the law apply to children in the land Down Under. We believe we exist in a democracy, but Australia is adept at child indifference. How long did it take for those children abused in institutions to get heard? Decades! The average age of the 8,000 victims (at the time of first abuse) was around 11. And tens of thousands of callers (victims of child sexual abuse) were outside the confined remit of *The Royal Commission into Institutional Responses to Child Sexual Abuse* and were never heard.

Though many good people strive to help and protect children who need help, on the flip side of the so-called 'protection' apparatus others are emboldened to use the system to exploit children because there is a monetary value in doing so. Tens of thousands of children have been betrayed by the State.

This book will hopefully provide an understanding of how society is being corroded by this exploitation of children. With over 46,000 children (0-17yrs) in Out-of-Home-Care[3], it's clear some children needed help -- but how many have been "deprived of their liberty"? Had they had "equal protection of the law" these kids would have escaped the lucrative "remove-and-place" State government (service industry) programs and still be at home with their parents (or carers) they love.

I will show you that Australia has participated in the cruel business of "stealing" children for three centuries, and I contend there is a 'protection racket' that has very little to do with the protection of children. With regard to the title of the book: the definition of a 'racket' is a fraudulent scheme, or activity; usually an illegitimate and lucrative enterprise made workable by intimidation and with immunity from prosecution, which I will attempt to demonstrate.

I have had to rush this book to print as desperate parents are pleading for assistance now to get their children back from the State. No court, minister, or oversight body will or can help them, and with each passing day the chances of parent-child reunion dwindles. These aggrieved parents display a connection with their children that is profound; a love that encompasses and envelops their entire existence. Their lives and the lives of their children have been shattered and something has to be done.

Some have suggested I remove my passion in the writing of this book. Sorry, but I have been unable to do this, as those people in government positions posing as protectors, but participating in the wrongfully removal of children, are simply racketeers.

For the children who have been unwarrantedly and unlawfully separated from their parents!

Abbreviations and Acronyms

ACIS - Acute Community Intervention Service

AFP - Australian Federal Police

A-G – Attorney-general

ALECOMM -- Australian Legislative Ethics Commission

ALRC -- Australian Law Reform Commission

APHRA – Australian Health Practitioner Association

AO – Order of Australia

CARL -- Child Abuse Report Line

CDPP - Commonwealth Director of Public Prosecutions

CPS - Child Protection Services

CRIC – Child Removal industrial Complex

CYPS - The Children's and Young People's Safety Act, 2017

DCP - Department for Child Protection

DHHS - Department of Health and Human Services

FACS (DCJ) NSW Department of Communities and Justice

FC – Family Court

FLA - The Family Law Act 1975 (Cth)

ICAC - Independent Commission Against Corruption, SA

ICCPR - International Covenant on Civil and Political Rights

ICL - Independent Child Lawyer

IIS - Internal Investigation Service, SAPOL

JCC - The Judicial Conduct Commissioner

MRM -- Monitoring and Reporting Mechanism

OOHC - Out-of-Home-Care

OPI - Office of Public Integrity

PAS -- Parent Alienation Syndrome

SAPOL - South Australian Police

UNCRC - UN Convention on the Rights of the Child

Contents

Part Three – Mechanics of Trading

Part Four – Insanities & Stranger Things

"History will have to record that the greatest tragedy of this period of social transition was not the strident clamor of the bad people, but the appalling silence of the good people... He who passively accepts evil is as much involved in it as he who helps to perpetrate it. He who accepts evil without protesting against it is really cooperating with it." --*Martin Luther King, Jr.*

Foreword – by Pastor Paul Robert Burton

When Dee emailed me a first draft of her new book *"The Child Protection Racket - High Level Child Trafficking In Australia"* and asked if I would read it and consider providing her a foreword, I said *"It would be an absolute honour"*.

I downloaded the draft PDF onto my trusty iPad and began reading it whilst flying with my partner from Newcastle to Brisbane. As an interesting aside we were flying up to assist as support persons (or so I thought as I was later escorted by security from the building) for Russell Pridgeon, Patrick O'Dea and a grandmother whom I can't name without risk of incarceration because her grandchild, who disclosed sexual abuse, was removed from her and returned to the alleged abuser.

Welcome to the Australian judicial system designed not to protect children, but to protect and enable the abusers of children.

Having developed significant speed reading skills from assisting around 150 parents over the last six and a half years in these places they call courts, all fighting for their children that had been removed by the various State and Territory Governments, I had already completed reading Part One "My Journey into Hell" before my Virgin economy flight had even left the ground.

My entire body was covered in goose bumps from head to toe. The more I read the more I thought to myself finally someone has refined, defined and created a true master piece exposing what happens when children become nothing more than "financial units" for a sick corrupt system, and why Australia now leads the world per capita for State and Federal Government Condoned Child Trafficking and Child Abuse.

This book uncovers the truth of a nation so far removed from "Australia The Lucky Country" that many may not want to believe what they are reading. This so called "Lucky Country" is still today, in 2023, engaged in a continued genocide of its indigenous population, and where racism abounds. This is a country where the child removal net has now grown much *much* wider and not only targets the indigenous but has now spread throughout our entire multicultural nation. And these child removal departments, by mid-2021, had in various capacities involved themselves in the lives of over 293,000 children nationally -- that's around 5.2% of all of our children.

It comes as no surprise that Dee has a substantive history as an accomplished film director, producer, book writer and investigative journalist, who hails from Southern Africa, having experienced the horrors of the apartheid in her youth. She has historically directed films including *The Second Jungle Book, Running Wild, Deadly Chase,* and was nominated and won Best Film and Script at the 2007 Inside Film Awards for her critically acclaimed film *The Jammed,* a film exposing human trafficking and the sex trade in Melbourne.

Here again she applies that same dedication and forensic journalistic approach characteristic of her art, to guide the reader through this "kids for cash" system exposing all who profit from it and shining a bright light in the darkness of secret closed courts and the associated court suppression laws that hide it all from the eyes and ears of the general public.

That is, until recently…

Thanks to the work of an amazing group of people in whom I have the greatest respect, that includes the wonderful Dee McLachlan and others, that form part of a tireless, dedicated national alliance of passionate volunteers. A group of volunteers that often put their own lives at risk to expose to you, the general public, the shocking TRUTH of what is happening to thousands and thousands of families and their children right under your noses.

It's the "Perfect Storm." The Out of Home Care system profits (using of course the National Disability Insurance Scheme), the medical professionals profit, the courts profit, the lawyers profit, the court appointed psychologists profit, the jails profit, and the police and the government benefits as the multi-national corporations providing these products and services work with them to ensure the legislation protects them all from being exposed -- at the expense of these poor hapless families and their children.

I hope this book by shining the bright light of truth in the darkness of pure evil can in some small way assist to bring about the substantive change we all wish to see in the world, and I commend not just Dee for this book and her efforts, but all the true spiritual warriors everywhere on this planet (recognizing this is a global issue) working so tirelessly to bring about the undeniable positive change so desperately needed at this time.

After all ... "it's all about the children and we should look upon ALL children as we do our own children."

Kindest Regards & God Bless

Paul

PART ONE

My Journey Looking into Hell

"Children are the living messages we send to a time we will not see." — *John F. Kennedy*

Baptism of Fire

This book is my journey of learning after being taken to the window that overlooked souls living in a hell ... on earth.

I was fortunate to be brought up in a caring and politically aware family and this nourished a positive and hopeful vision for humanity. I'm familiar with how a police state operates, and even as a child I acquired an understanding of how one group of humans could apply cruel rules and wield unjust laws on another. I was born in South Africa, and grew up under the 'Apartheid regime'. It was dehumanizing and inhumane for non-whites, and I felt ashamed of my home country back then. I now feel ashamed of Australia as it fails children while protecting the unfettered powers of an inhumane regime.

I have a global barometer; I served briefly in the army, went to university, and was fortunate to explore, live and work in many parts of the world -- the UK, US, Europe, Argentina, Sudan, Namibia, Botswana, Zimbabwe, Kenya, Philippines, Sri Lanka are some. I am not unfamiliar with impoverished communities surviving harsh conditions -- yet they resonated with laughter and a connectedness to life and family. I've immigrated three times; lived in California for seven years, settling in Melbourne, Australia in 1999. I wanted to be part of the "we are one and free" in a land "abound in nature's gifts." I joyfully believed in "Advance Australia Fair" and that I was living in one of the most idyllic countries on the planet.

But, in mid-September 2018 that changed.

I was filming Rachel Vaughan in South Australia when it was suggested we both meet this mother. She had a story to tell, and I met her on the same day the South Australian Youth Court awarded guardianship of her daughter to the State. Her daughter had been forcibly removed through a deception – and in violation to Federal Family Court orders less than three months after the mum had been awarded sole custody by Family Court. After a nine-day trial, the Federal jurisdiction had affirmed that she was the safe responsible parent, but a few months later the lower State court abrogated the order. In defiance of the Family Court orders (that stated the child shall not be removed from her mother's care), the child protection agencies and police fabricated evidence and made false submissions to claim the mother was a danger.

It was sheer trickery on every level.

My few days in Adelaide was a baptism of fire – firstly, hearing about Rachel's historical accounts of being sexually abused as a child, witnessing murders, and being trafficked by her father; and secondly, meeting this mum (I'll call her Joanne Doe) and hearing her present-day abduction story.

I struggled to understand why such a caring and competent mother had lost her daughter to the State and firmly believed that the government, on being shown, would correct their mistake. It took some time to realize that their actions were orchestrated and deliberate; that this was a business; that the child protection system is not broken, but rather a well-oiled machine and service industry specializing in 'child removals' on a mass scale.

For four years I wrote hundreds of letters (backed up by phone calls) to the Department for Child Protection (DCP), to Ministers, the Ombudsman, Commissioners, to the Guardian, to SAPOL (South Australian Police) and their Internal Investigation Service (IIS); to the Prime Minister(s), Governors, and to all the judicial and corruption oversight bodies that I could find (ICAC, OPI, JCC, etc.). No one was willing to help ... or perhaps, no one was *able* to help. It was all lip service with the government seemingly impotent in being able to assist a child that had been taken (judicially abducted) from the person she most loved in the world.

Over time, my bright view of Australia evaporated. I began to consider that little has changed in the Australian psyche since those days of the penal colony. We have a grim convict history, shipping about 164,000 convicts to Australia between 1788 and 1868 using the British government's *Transportation Act 1717*. Approximately 25,000 convict women, most likely 'exported' to balance the gender scales, were charged with petty crimes and sent to places like the Cascades Female Factory, a damp distillery-cum-prison in Van Diemen's Land (Tasmania). Thousands of children were 'exported' Down Under, and as Steve Harris (*The Lost Boys of Mr Dickens*) writes: "As many as 25,000 were under 18, with between 10,000 and 13,000 young boys dispatched to Van Diemen's Land".[4]

The distribution of humans, as a resource, (e.g., convicts or slaves) was (and is) motivated by economics for the 'corporate' elite. For example, before *The Slavery Abolition Act* of 1833, *The Slave Trade Act 1807* (UK) made the purchase or ownership of slaves illegal within the British Empire with the exception of the territories under the *East India Company* (a private corporation).

Nothing much has changed – only the offices, the laws and the final destination. As an analogy, consider the aforementioned 25,000 children exported to Australia over 80 years. That's only about 312 children a year (on average). Presently in 2023, thousands of children and infants are removed from their homes every year -- removed by State child 'protection' departments (with approximately 61,000 children under care and protection orders; that's about 11 per 1000 children).

It may be that many public servants genuinely seek to protect vulnerable children, but under a cloak of authority and secrecy others engage in openly dishonest and questionable practices. How many children have been removed unwarrantedly or unlawfully is unknown. However, it's clear that the Australian Child 'Protection' system is not only a booming business, but

…it's become a racket!

A Journey of Understanding

When I first began this journey I naively thought my efforts would lead to justice. But what unfolded demonstrated that established 'protection' systems and institutions that were to supposedly help Australian children were either (a) irreparably broken or dysfunctional, or (b) designed to facilitate a service industry. There is a third option: that the flawed appearance of the child 'protection' system is a cover for the business of 'removals'.

I wrote my first article in Gumshoe News on this subject in September 2018 and was immediately flooded with emails and calls from desperate parents. I had made the movie, *The Jammed*, in 2006, inspired by true stories on sex trafficking in Melbourne, but I was unprepared for this type of trafficking. The stories I was told were heartbreaking and overwhelming, and inspired me to do a survey – which I outline in more detail later in the book.

After this initial realization, my journey drifted through the five stages of grief: At first I was in *denial*. I could not believe that people would act so abhorrently, and thought the unwarranted removal of Joanne's daughter (and others) could be rectified -- but it was not to be. After listening to many similar cases, I became extremely *angry* when I had the realization that these actions by government seemed deliberate. Through 2019 and 2020 I was in the *bargaining* phase, writing hundreds of documents and letters, publishing articles and ghost-writing legal action and books – setting my film career and earnings aside.

As time passed the hopelessness of challenging the power structures and the sheer depth of the corruption and bureaucratic indifference sent me into a state of *depressed* indignation. I lost faith in humanity. In late-2022, I woke up one morning reflecting on how the 'war' against children has been raging for millennia. I reached *acceptance* that this is humanity's dark journey. We are a predatory species and trading and using children as a resource has always been (whether for money, slavery, war, sacrifice, Satanism, pedophilia, or adrenochrome).

The regurgitated mantra that in modern democratic societies "…there are legal frameworks, human rights conventions, and advocacy efforts dedicated to protecting children from exploitation, abuse, and any form of harm," is a sham – a complete nonsense. Nothing could be further from the truth for the children of those parents who have contacted me. Their children were either: unwarrantedly removed; unlawfully "abducted" by the State; "stolen"; "judicially kidnapped"; traded or "trafficked" by the "Cash for Kids" child trade industry. You can choose later.

The statutes, case law, and common law are still on the books, but are ignored by the court officials and public servants.

We've published over 170 articles on this topic on Gumshoe News (gumshoenews.com), many written by me, but this seems to make no difference -- except to inspire the court or Crown to further intimidate a parent. Many parents, children, and others have exposed this agenda – and many have been punished for doing so (e.g., Pastor Paul's s105 challenge and the Pridgeon | O'Dea case are discussed later in the book).

And what I am telling you is not new. US Georgia Senator (2004-2008) Nancy Schaefer spoke out on the corruption in Child Protective Services (CPS)[5]. At a conference in 2008, she said, "…child protective services have become a protected empire built on taking children and separating families." She and her husband were undoubtedly murdered (by "suicide").

This *is* a war against family, parents (father and motherhood) and their children. I hold this book out to you – like a lit candle to shine a light on humanity (in Australia). You can either choose to read on and do something… or blow the candle out. If you do choose the latter, you are blowing out the candle in your own soul.

"Human [child] trafficking is the physical movement of people across and within borders through deceptive means, force or coercion. The people who commit human trafficking offences are motivated by the continuing exploitation of their victims..."[6] *Australian Federal Police*

PART TWO

Australia is expert at "stealing" children.

"To be well adjusted to a profoundly sick society is no measure of health"

The 'Stealing Children' Business

Australia participated in the trade of 'importing' so-called convict children (as young as 13) from Britain and Ireland. The suspicion of petty larceny (theft under one shilling) was enough to send you packing. Australia was paid to take them, and children were expected to work on arrival. This human resource transfer was facilitated by the *Transportation Act 1717*, from around 1788 to 1868.

Then in 1869, coincidentally, the focus turned to the First Nations peoples, with the '*Act to provide for the Protection and Management of the Aboriginal Natives of Victoria*'. The state (of Victoria) had already prepared the way through *The Neglected and Criminal Children's Act* 1864 (No.216) -- the first piece of legislation in Victoria to define how children might be removed from their parents. The 1869 Act was later amended to the *Aborigines Act 1890*.[7] "This new legislation continued the Protection Board's power to remove children to and from 'stations' [missions...], orphanages... [etc.]" Stolen Generation testimonials give some idea of the calamitous so-called 'protection' outcomes:

> "You're going to be here for the rest of your life, like the rest of us... You won't see your mother anymore." (Netta, *Stolen Generation Stories*[8])

The authorized power, the 'Protection' Board, did everything but protect. (Note the incongruous use of the word 'protection'.) The country was expert at "stealing" children, legally; and yes, can now refer to these children as being 'stolen'. Oh, be heartened though (*cough*): in 2008 Prime Minister Kevin Rudd gave a formal apology to the "Stolen Generations" whose lives "had been blighted by past government policies of forced child removal" from their families from the mid-1800s to the 1970s.

But like an infomercial: *wait there's more!*

From the 1920s to 1970s, under the Child Migrant Program (a population-labour scheme) more than 130,000 children were sent to a "better life" in former colonies, mainly Australia and Canada. Mostly sourced from deprived families, the fortunes of these children aged between three and 14 varied. Many suffered lonely and brutal childhoods.

And as one scheme abated, another child "remove-and-place" program replaced it.

I quote from Victoria's DHHS (Department of Health and Human Services) records.[9] "During the 1950s and 1960s, the community services sector experimented with foster care" in the general population, with concerted publicity campaigns to recruit foster carers through the 1960s. "By the 1970s foster care was defined as a service enabling the placement of a child or children with a selected family for a planned period while work occurred with the natural family towards the child's return home or to a permanent placement." I'm sure there were serious attempts to improve the lives of children in the general population (to phase out orphanages and institutions, and children neglected at home) -- but like the old proverb, "The road to hell is paved with good intentions." Corrosive concepts and ideals would override good intentions into exploitation.

By the 1970s, 'child protection' had moved on from the First Nations to protecting all children. *The Children and Young Persons (Care and Protection) Act* (157/1998) provided "for the care and protection of, and the provision of services to, children…" and this created the contemporary systems we know. *The Child Protection Act 1999* (Qld) outlined "best interests" of the child as the main principle. Sadly, in so many instances, it seems the courts functioned on "worst interests."

In the mid-70s, *The Family Law Act 1975* (Cth) (FLA) set out how to manage custody and "child protection concerns" in Federal Family Law courts. This initiated a legal mechanism to settle custody disputes through an adversarial court process. There's a jurisdictional twist with regard to the 'protection' of children. Family Court (Federal legislation) is the superior jurisdiction, but in Australia it is subservient to the State courts when it comes to child protection and State child protection orders. This is through s69ZK of the *Family Law Act 1975,* where nothing in the Act affects the operation of a child welfare law in relation to a child. This means that the lower Children's Courts have the "controlling interests" in the trade of children. Maybe you haven't grasped this concept yet, but it will soon become clear.

The child removal departments use the law, as governments did before them over hundreds of years, to remove children. And, they have the words "protection" and "safety" to guile you. For example, The Department for Child Protection SA (DCP) uses *The Children's and Young People's Safety Act,* 2017 (CYPS Act) to abduct a child from families, and from the federally ordered and lawful care of mothers and fathers.

When I was riding around the central desert of Australia, I spoke to an emergency nurse about this book. She explained her experience with child protection services was the opposite of what I was describing. When, as a mandatory reporter, she'd come across a child in need of help (rescue) she'd make a report. She said nothing was ever done, and that the department would only act for that child after six of seven serious reports. (When I say "department", I am referring to the child protection department of that specific State.) Why would public servants (social workers) do absolutely nothing in some serious cases -- yet in others intervene aggressively to claim guardianship of a child on the flimsiest of information? I find this puzzling, but essentially the outcome for the child is irrelevant as this is just a business.

This chapter is about the 'child stealing' business, and how society, government and the law have presented this as acceptable practice. It's not acceptable and makes the *Bringing Them Home* report in 1997 and the 2008 "sorry" apology to the Stolen

Generations a farce. Has the Stolen Generation ended? The NSW FACS (the Department of Communities and Justice, DCJ) Annual Report 2019-2020 under the section[10], *2.6 'Children and families thrive'* states:

> "During 2019–20, caseworkers brought 2,206 children into care... This included 952 Aboriginal children, an increase of 2.4 per cent as compared with 2018–19."

The use of "thrive" is interesting! 952 Aboriginal children out of 2,206 were brought into care in one year? That's 43% of children from only 3.4% of people in NSW who identified as Aboriginal and/or Torres Strait Islander in the 2021 Census.

Thus, are the anecdotal stories I have been told true?

Pastor Paul Robert Burton has researched this for many years and has detailed how certain agencies have gone into Aboriginal communities to vacuum up 20 to 30 children over a long week-end as if they were on a self-endorsed quota system. Is this a revised contemporary version of the 'stolen generation'? I also recently received a substack post[11] by Josephine Cashman that read (extract[12]):

> "I'm a whistle-blower. I served under 2 Prime Ministers providing independent advice. I uncovered a child trafficking and drug supply network. Resulting in child suicides, caused by an untouchable government funded crook of the Uluru Voice Con. The Aboriginal communities were blocked from reporting the crimes locally. They asked me to take their concerns to Canberra. I asked the Government to speak with the Australian Crime Commission and the Australian Federal Police about it. Immediately after this the government and the media went after me. They tried to set me up. They tried to discredit me..."

The Default Solution

The government's default solution for "protection" or "safe" is to "remove the child."

It is also almost impossible to obtain details and reasons for why specific children were taken into care as the child departments and children's courts operate in complete SECRECY. Presently, there are about 50,000 children (0-18y) in State Out-of-Home-Care (OOHC) – which includes foster care, kinship care, and residential care. And the industry is growing annually; faster than population growth.

Obviously, there are children at risk; they might have drugged out parents; or are surviving in a home that has alarming accounts of domestic violence, sexual assault or neglect. The mainstream media often publishes these accounts of neglectful parents – but rarely stories of unwarranted removals.

There are also many struggling or problematic parents who fail to offer good homes for some reason, but with some support these parents could get back on their feet. And helping these families should be the more effective and preferred outcome rather than a blanket 'removals-removals' policy. There are some encouraging actions, as described in the NSW FACS Annual Report 2019-2020[13] to keep families together where possible "...to support children to remain safely at home and to prevent them from entering OOHC..." by providing 380 places in a Permanency Support Program.

The problem of children in care is that the government turns out to be a BAD PARENT... over and over again. Their own statistics reveal children taken into government care are more likely to be harmed; their families are disrupted and the child's potential stunted. It's like removing the child from the frying pan into the fire.

It's also generational – the children of parents who have survived the system will often become future "clients."

I met this young woman and her mother when I was in the SA's Youth Court waiting area. She was hoping the judge would order her weeks-old baby back into her care. I asked her why they had taken her new-born only 3 hours after she was born. She said she had been in the "system" as a 13-year-old after being removed from her mother – against her will. It did not take long for her, as a teen, to be repeatedly raped (something that would never have happened in her mum's care, she said). A few years later, she was involved in an incident where she fought off her boyfriend in an argument. Despite her claiming self-defence, a report was made against her. Life moved on and a few years later she fell pregnant. As soon as she gave birth, social workers from the department (DCP) appeared, and using the historical incident against her, removed her newborn for its 'safety'. Clearly, they have ways to source and track their generational clients.

I don't recall the women's name, and I often wonder if the DCP ever considered returning her baby and allowing her the miracle of motherhood which she desired; or whether this baby was 'farmed out' into the system until 18-years of age.

I also have suspicions that the child departments have two sets of books – those reported in their records, and then those off-books kids that get "lost" in the system. We have no way to find out, and if a child in the system goes "missing" he or she would be impossible to trace. The *Children and Young People (Safety) Act* 2017 gives discretion to the Chief Executive to change a name and "disappear" a child into the system (for their safety).

A friend had told me about someone who had witnessed babies being sold out of the boot of a car. But this witness was fearful of speaking out and a requested conversation with this man never eventuated. (But more about baby 'harvesting' later.)

The Racket Exposed

A lot of people are making large sums of money through the culture of 'removals'. And the system, regardless of its legality, can be maliciously cruel and dehumanizing. Many of us believe it is designed this way – designed to be cruel to children and families. And when public servants and the judiciary act beyond their powers, and/or unlawfully, they thus participate in exploitation or abduction.

I contend this child trade or 'protection racket' operates like a syndicate with each person playing their role.

Syndicates form alliances to pool resources effectively where each syndicate partner shoulders some of the risk of any potential negative impacts if a transaction (child removal) runs into trouble. Each profession, department or person is a cog in the wheel facilitating the smooth (legal and illegal) removal of children from unsuspecting families and vulnerable parents. As each person (e.g., social worker, supervisor, police officer, psychologist, psychiatrist, doctor, family consultant, department Executive, Independent child lawyer, department's legal team, magistrate, etc.) only performs their role so no one is wholly accountable. Like layers of an onion, one profession shields the next making it almost impossible to challenge, with vulnerable parents being unable to comprehend the scale and ingenuity of the removals business.

I believe the principles of predation in the wild apply here too. The 'predators' are adverse to risk-threat and so hone in on the weak and vulnerable. I met a young foreign-born couple who had their three children removed on medical grounds regarding the one child. The claim was spurious. They were smart, resourced, had family support, and the mother was a nurse. They challenged quickly and efficiently, and with the support of the foster carer got their children back. Had this been another struggling single mum I am sure she would have lost all her children for good.

Once the department has possession of a child, it is easy for the lies and delinquency (misconduct) to compound -- as one misstatement evolves into a complex fabrication. It becomes a rendition of 'Chinese whispers'. Often the department staffs work as a relay team (as they did in Joanne's case). The first case worker (that removes the child) creates an accusation from a suspicion, for example, that the mother suffers from some undiagnosed mental health condition. Worker #1 then passes the baton to the next case worker who inherits the spurious suspicion and modifies this into an assumption and treats the mother accordingly. After a year or so, when a third case worker is assigned, the original suspicion has morphed into a 'fact' (that the mother *has* a mental health condition despite assessments clearing her of any issues).

The forced removal of a child from a mother is traumatizing as the natural biological and psychological bonds are severed. The fact that a mother's love is the underpinning of us as a healthy species is set aside. The mother's distress and trauma, instead, becomes the fertile ground for accusations of degrading mental health issues. How ignominious! In so many cases the action of the department (removing the children) is actually the CAUSE of any of the parent's problems (e.g., PTSD). This harm to the parent is then twisted later to justify separation and guardianship.

By the time the (delayed) matter is heard in court, the magistrate or judge is often offered a scrambled and deceitful account of the facts; and with his or her alignment with the 'removals culture' it's easy to justify awarding the child to the state.

The default reasoning is to remove the child, so in many cases it's just 'RUBBER STAMPING' -- "Next!" The sheer might and financial resources of the government so heavily outweighs any parent. I heard about a young mum collapsing outside the courtroom; sobbing, and begging for the magistrate to allow her parents in as support. It was denied. The magistrate had said (sarcastically) something like, "You have a voice; you're not mentally impaired are you?" In the waiting room, the young mum's parents were egging her on trying to break through her anxiety. "Get in there an' go and save your baby." I would bet that the mother never did. You see, in Children's or Youth court, the single parent enters the court (generally) alone. She (or he) might have a legal team – but usually legal aid lawyers will not want to "upset" the court. They have been indoctrinated into the removals culture, and very often betray their clients. On the other side are the Crown's well-resourced legal team and the child's legal team. Everyone in court wants to stay on the government-sponsored gravy train – so they default to facilitating the child department's wishes; plus the legal profession seems acclimatized to the removals process. Whether this is through being co-opted, conditioned, habituated, or indoctrinated is a question for debate. Several courageous lawyers have lost their licenses for challenging the thinking and processes of these 'star chambers'.

In other cases, the criminality is just blatant. Public servants from the police and child departments will manipulate statements, write fake reports, conceal evidence, and perjure themselves to remove a child. (I present evidence of this later.) The psych professionals will write reports-to-order, and no oversight body (or APHRA) dares to crack down on the 'protection racket' – i.e., the business of trading children.

A twist in the law provides a haven for the 'protection racket'. I contend that, as I will show, a 22-year-old social worker (child welfare officer) with minimal experience and who is *not* a mother, has more power over your child than the Child Minister, the Governor of the State, the Prime Minister, and the Federal High Courts.

With regard to unlawful removals, I refer you to one case where some brave activists and advocates, Pastor Paul Robert Burton and Dr Andrew Katelaris in Newcastle, managed to get a disabled child back to his parents after a two year grueling battle in court. For two years the disabled child was kept in a residential hotel room, deprived of love and parental contact, supervised by 2 workers rotating through 24 hour cycles. He was not properly cared for, and his exploitation cost the taxpayer millions, and made huge amounts of money for the organization that was paid to look after him. Paul and Andrew have been subjected to six years of the judicial system (for speaking out) – charged for six years for having violated Sec 105 of The *NSW Children and Young Persons Care and Protection Act*, in revealing on Facebook the name of a child-in-trouble – while 4 million others did too. They bravely exposed DOCS/FACS/DCJ, the NSW child department, and how the child was removed on May 19th 2017 -- without delegated authority and on KNOWN FALSE grounds.[14]

Australia is expert at removing children from families. And it is by design. This, of course, is at odds with what is published on government websites, such as *The Australian Institute of Health and Welfare* (AIHW) which states[15], "Child protection refers to preventing and responding to violence, exploitation, abuse, neglect, and harmful practices against children (UNICEF 2021). …Child protection functions to protect the fundamental rights of children which include safety, freedom from violence and a stable family environment (UN General Assembly 1989). …The child protection system aims to protect children from maltreatment in family settings… It includes all types of physical and/or emotional ill-treatment, sexual abuse, neglect, negligence and commercial or other exploitation, which results in actual or potential harm to the child's health, survival, development or dignity…"

This may be true for some children, but unfortunately, it is the government that is emotionally abusing, neglecting, commercially exploiting, and exposing thousands of children to greater risk of sexual abuse when they remove a child from a loving family on hearsay or erroneous grounds.

It is the government through enforced 'removals' that potentially harms the child's social development and dignity.

Non-application of the Law

The requirement outlined in S65AA of the *Family Law Act* 1975, says "A court must have regard to the best interests of the child as the paramount consideration" (also referenced in many of the articles in the UNCRC). In State child protection laws the safety of the child is the paramount consideration. But I now believe Australian children have NO rights. They are not listened to, and have little or no say on their lives. The Conventions and Treaties Australia has signed to protect children are meaningless.

In this chapter, I'll introduce the issue of child sexual abuse, as this is one of the mechanisms designed to remove a child from a parent. And this applies to both Family and Children's courts. Good you may say -- the child needs to be protected. But maybe you have gathered by now that the definition of "protection" does not mean "the act of protecting; from harm or injury." Remember, we are talking about a 'protection racket'. The antonym of protection is exposed; uncertainty, unprotected from harm. So, when a report of child sexual abuse is made, in many cases the child will NOT be protected. In Family Court, the judge will regularly remove the child from the protective parent and award custody to the abuser. In children's court the protective parent will be accused of being the psychological abuser or coacher resulting in the child becoming a ward of the state. (A woman in QLD has just been jailed for going on the run in an attempt to protect her children after reports of alleged abuse.)

A WARNING to any parents out there: if you report child sexual abuse in Australia, there is a likelihood that *you* will lose your children. (You need to seek the right help.) To the normal person this sounds so bizarre and nonsensical. Yes, it is totally deranged. And if a child discloses abuses (e.g., rape) to his/her grandparents, parent, or to a psychologist or doctor, it is likely the child will NOT be believed by magistrates and judges. In many cases the child's legal representative, the ICL (Independent Child Lawyer) will go against the children (their clients) too.

At first I thought that these judicial officers (in both family and children's courts) were either totally ignorant or had no apperception of what the child or children had gone through. But the more cases I reviewed, the more I began to think that their bizarre actions were following a script or a business protocol. That may not be true but it seems that way. Would you return a child back into the care of a person that had 40 mandatory reports of sexual abuse against them? (Shane Dowling[16] has questioned whether judges and magistrates are protecting pedophiles.) I am sure some children's court judges do believe some children were abused, but they often act as if they did not. It seems that their default solution is to discredit sexual abuse; so does this mean that they do not believe that child rape is harmful to the child? Or is there something else at play?

As in Joanne's case, I often wondered why everybody, in unison, took the side of those public servants who had acted so criminally. (Why would the government try place a child back with their alleged abuser when the law dictates "safety is paramount..."?) Many people claim these agencies and the courts have been infiltrated with Freemasons; and that their secret allegiance to protect their brethren overrides their duties to a court of law.

Another legal quandary is that the rules of evidence do not apply in the family and children's courts, and the words of a Court Report Writer (a psychologist who might have never met the child) override facts and evidence.

No one seems to follow the law. Sec 60CI of the *Family Law Act* 1975 (1)(b) requires State or Territory agencies to inform the court of any "notification, report, investigation, inquiry or assessment relating to abuse, or an allegation, suspicion or risk of abuse." But this is often ignored, with judges regularly ordering that the evidence of sexual abuse be destroyed. *Inconceivable!* (A judge would never dispose of evidence in a tax fraud case.)

I have evidence that a number of South Australian state laws were broken in order to remove children from mothers. The *Children and Young People (Safety) Act* 2017 should provide a foundation for the protection of children, but this was being used AGAINST children. Youth Court judges and magistrates twisted the law to suit the department, not the child. s58—Standard of proof... "is to be proved on the balance of probabilities," but they balance the scales. Hearsay or opinion outweighs evidence allowing Children's and Youth courts to become 'Star chambers'.

The Interagency Code of Practice (ICOP) requires that the child must always be listened to, believed, and investigated before anything else. But, the department ignores this. (I covered much of this in video series: www.youtube.com/@childabduction2935) In one South Australian case, a number of public servants did not listen or investigate but acted criminally believing they were immune to any wrongdoing. In fact, the protection laws were used to 'protect' a sexual perpetrator, and not the child. I presented facts and evidence to ministers and oversight agencies that these laws below (as per the *Criminal Law Consolidation Act* (1935) SA) were broken by police officers and department staff:

> s241 (1) (2) (a) "impeding investigation of the offence; or (b) assisting the principal offender to escape apprehension or prosecution... of the offence...";

> s242 (2) is when a person "counsels, procures, induces, aids or abets another to make a false statement under oath is guilty of subornation of perjury";

> s243 (a) "...concealing (or destroying) anything that may be required in evidence at judicial proceedings..."; (d) "influencing the outcome of judicial proceedings..."

> s251 (1) "A public officer who improperly—(b) ...fails to discharge or perform an official duty or function; or (e) causing injury or detriment to another person..."

s14--Criminal Neglect-- requires everyone (1)(d) "to take steps that he or she could reasonably be expected to have taken in the circumstances to protect the victim [child] from harm..."

Div 8—142 (2) "A person is guilty of an offence if the person dishonestly exploits an advantage to which this section applies in order to— (a) benefit him/herself or another; or (b) cause a detriment to another"; and

s80—(1) Abduction of child under 16y, states "Any person who (a) unlawfully, either by force or fraud...(c) to deprive any parent, guardian or other person, having the lawful care of the child... shall be guilty...[liable to be imprisoned]..."

The Chief Executive of the DCP (Cathy Taylor at the time), not only caused detriment to these parents, but this resulted in suicide(s). Pastor Paul was supporting one of those mothers. They often remove children and deprive parents of their lawful care and possession of their children on specious grounds. One mum presently communicating with me has not seen her 4-year-old son for 150 days. But imagine how the young lad's feeling. His whole world was his mother and it took three officers to tear him away.

How could these people act with such cruelty?

Australia ratified the Convention on *The Rights of The Child* on 17 December 1990[17]. Article 3-- all organizations concerned with children should work towards what is best for each child; Article Article 9— Children should not be separated from their parents except... [when] separation is necessary for the best interests of the child, and article 19-- Governments should ensure that children are properly cared for and protect them from violence, abuse and neglect by their parents, or anyone else who looks after them (but statistics demonstrate the government is a bad parent).

It's diabolical -- and there's really no word in the thesaurus that comes close to those describing the suffering caused.

The Science of Harm

The actions of forcibly removing a child from the parent/s are traumatic and disorientating, and the consequences of separating a child from a loving relationship are one of the most extreme forms of psychological abuse to the child. Would a child be able to distinguish a forced removal experience from a kidnapping?

Paediatrics professor Charles Nelson from Harvard Medical School in the USA spoke about this in a Washington Post article,[18] entitled, "What separation from parents does to children: 'The effect is catastrophic'."

> "This is what happens inside children when they are forcibly separated from their parents. Their heart rate goes up. Their body releases a flood of stress hormones such as cortisol and adrenaline. Those stress hormones can start killing off dendrites — the little branches in brain cells that transmit messages. In time, the stress can start killing off neurons and, especially in young children, wreaking dramatic and long-term damage, both psychologically and to the physical structure of the brain.
>
> "The effect is catastrophic," said Charles Nelson... "There's so much research on this that if people paid attention at all to the science, they would never do this."

Some children need rescuing and removal might brief relief. But because some children were rescued from screwed up parents, does not justify the extensive collateral damage to ALL the other children through this policy. Yet "removal" is the DEFAULT government solution – i.e., use an extreme form of abuse to resolve the possibility of abuse. This book refers to the thousands of children that were screaming or pleading to remain in their home (or placement). Consider for a moment police raiding *your* home and forever dispatching you, against your will, to a strange location away from your loved ones. You'd be forever changed

41

and traumatized (and you'd be seeking compensation). These are calamitous and "catastrophic" actions that consistently ripple into Australia's future generations.

> "Even very brief separations are harmful to infants and young children. Our sympathetic nervous system kicks in and impels us to try cope with this separation by crying… [etc]. Then comes a flood or cortisol (stress hormone); prolonged exposure can be harmful as it begins to damage brain cells. Hippocampal cells will die – that's our memory centre; the electric activity in the brain is reduced by prolonged separations." *Karlen Lyons-Ruth*, psychologist Cambridge Hospital.[19]

> "Not only does it affect the architecture of the brain, but long-term it effects health and early death" *Robin Deutsch,* William James College, on the Amygdala.

Many monkey experiments demonstrate the deleterious effects of child-mother separation and how it might impair socialization and development. There is also a legal precedent of the lifelong consequences of separation. Sir James Munby explained the gravity in family cases or a child subject to care proceedings in *Re J (A Child) [2013] EWHC 2694 (Fam)* (paragraph 28)[20], stating,

> "I have said this many times in the past but it must never be forgotten that, with the state's abandonment of the right to impose capital sentences, orders of the kind which family judges are typically invited to make in public law proceedings are amongst the most drastic that any judge in any jurisdiction is ever empowered to make. When a family judge makes a placement order or an adoption order in relation to a twenty-year old mother's baby, the mother will have to live with the consequences of that decision for what may be upwards of 60 or even 70 years, and the baby for what may be upwards of 80 or even 90 years. We must be vigilant to guard against the risks."

Addicted to Cruelty?

In trying to assist the rescue of this one child over several years, all my attempts to seek compassion, justice and restitution from our leaders fell on deaf or indifferent ears and closed doors. A very small number of officials did write back, such as the Hon Steve Irons (assistant minister to the Prime Minister, 2019) showing genuine concern and writing on to the Attorney-general.

A few parents have described how their experience with the child protection agencies, and children's or family courts was analogous to the Stanford Prison Experiment.[21] In 1971 twenty-four random university students were selected to enact guards and prisoners in the basement of Stanford University. Psychologist Professor Phillip Zimbrano wanted to explain the inherent traits of both guards and prisoner, but after six days he had to halt the experiment. He noted that around one third of the guards, young men randomly chosen, exhibited genuine sadistic tendencies. This experiment is often "held up as proof that most people can inflict cruelty and suffering on another human being if they are given a position of power and ordered to do so."[22] (And I suggest the sadistic traits in women would be much the same?)

I contend the Australian Federal and State governments are hooked on the service economy of exploiting children; i.e., 'child removals'. Put simply, it's "Jobs and Growth." It's now a multi-billion dollar asset to the economy, but I characterize it as a malignancy that erodes the very fabric of society through the destruction of family and father/motherhood. Over a few years, South Australia's former Child Protection Minister Rachel Sanderson ignored our countless pleas to intervene for this one child. I presented proof of department misfeasance, but she was too busy handing out lollipops to age care residents[23] to consider the child's sexual abuse disclosures, or how she was unlawfully removal from her mother's care. I have to wonder, did Ms Sanderson intervene for any child in all the years she was minister?

In some ways, I feel pity for Ms Sanderson. I'm sure she was kept insulated from anything to do with child protection, and was placed into her ministerial post to be used as a photo-opportunity on occasion. She had to learn from the media that two teens under her care had been raped -- and this only came to light because they were pregnant.

As expected, I was still unable to initiate any action from the new SA minister's (Katrine Hildyard) office. Even though the staff tried to be more cooperative, the minister's position seems void of action; and I am still waiting for questions to be answered.

However, when Dr Russell Pridgeon wrote to child Minister Di Farmer in Queensland requesting her to intervene and assist with three children who had suffered sexual abuse he simply got the 'brick-wall-treatment'. Ms Farmer's office just blocked the good doctor's email addresses each time. Truly disgraceful! At least the minister could have replied, explaining, "I apologize, as the child protection minister, I have no powers or authority to protect children." To accept this cruelty and claim you are the "protector" of children is the gravest deceit. But Dr Pridgeon insists that they all know what's going on, and are complicit in this criminality.

As a society, our leaders need to come to terms with this addiction to the 'protection racket' and stop accepting cruel actions, flagrant corruption, and malfeasance as normal operating consequences. Let me cite an example of how authorities did not protect, but rather punished a child:

This child (I'll call her Ella) had disclosed sexual abuse (forms of torture, rape and "hurt") by her father and "others" to a number of professionals and to a police officer (over 3 years). But nothing was ever done. It was Friday around lunchtime, and her father was to pick her up after school for week-end visitation. Obviously frightened and realizing authorities were not helping her, the young girl then bravely spoke to a new teacher detailing some of the harrowing abuses and an injury she'd had recently suffered.

She told her teacher she was "scared" of going with her father and wanted to stay with her mum. The teacher was obligated to report the matter to CARL (Child Abuse Report Line).

This is like one of those pub tales: a teacher (and her pupil), a policewoman, and a school principal walk into a bar... The police woman, Officer C Thompson, had interviewed Ella months before and was that afternoon on the phone to the principal urging that the child be sent home with her father.

What happened to the police officer?

She was promoted. The officer had conducted an interview with Ella a few months before and wrote in her entries, "NIL DISCLOSURES". 20 months later it was discovered that she had concealed ALL of the child's sexual abuse disclosures (versions of rape) from CARL, CPS, the DCP, and from the courts. Curiously and conveniently, this officer was in place for the teacher's notification and ready to discredit the child (and her mother).

What happened to the teacher?

I read a note that indicated the Education Department obviously considered that listening to the child's sexual abuse disclosures was distressing for the staff member – so I believe the teacher was offered counselling and time off.

What happened to the child?

Ella was PUNISHED. She was removed from her protective mother, Joanne, for bravely speaking out. That afternoon the principal sent her home with her father; then later that night she was returned to her mother. But that was a temporary trick. Shortly after, the DCP, using a court order, removed Ella from her mother (on the basis no evidence of abuse existed). Ella has never been allowed to return to her home; and you know the saying: 'Possession is nine-tenths of the law'.

"Man is the cruelest animal."
— *Friedrich Nietzsche*

"All cruelty springs from weakness."
— *Seneca, Seneca's Morals*

Schadenfreude

I have been told accounts of social workers cheering and high-fiving in court when a child was removed from a despairing and sobbing mother. It appears that many people in the courts, some experts (e.g., psychologists), and a sector in the agencies act in the cruelest and most sadistic way.

I am still struggling to explain the sheer perniciousness of the actions by *some* child protection agency staff – and why they do this. Schadenfreude, a German word, is for someone experiencing pleasure, or self-satisfaction derived from witnessing the trauma or humiliation of others. I will also quote from Psychologytoday[24]:

"Freud believed that sadism, or the desire to cause pain to another human being, is the result of a mix of sexual desire and aggression …and are a natural part of human nature." Heinz Kohut… argued that sadistic behavior results from what he called "fragmentation," and "…author Christopher Bollas says that beneath hateful behavior lies a profound emptiness… he suggests, better to feel sadistic than not to feel at all." Gabriel Marcel originally coined the phrase, "The Spirit of Abstraction" as defining the practice of conceiving of people as *functions* rather than as human beings – whether they be slaves, or enemies at war.

I would say all the above, but some people seem to 'get off' on their unfettered power, and appear to be getting 'self-nourishment' through their actions in some form of energy or frequency transference. I suspect envy and jealousy may play a part. Many may have been sexually abused as children -- this stunting their emotions of empathy and compassion through past dissociated trauma. And what was done to them could invoke an impulse to inflict and deflect their trauma upon the next generation.

There are a few moments that reverberate in my memory. I recall the one meeting I had in early 2019 with a case worker and her supervisor – two women from the St Mary's DCP office, South

Australia (Ms Moses and Ms Talbot). I was there as a support person for Joanne, and it was clear the meeting was to discredit her mental health despite her having previously and effectually passed a number of mental health assessments. (As per the *modus operandi* of the relay team, case worker #1, Ms Cakebread, had already done her bit and had been moved on.)

When the meeting began, I knew we had a problem. Despite the Federal Family Court awarding Joanne sole custody, the supervisor suggested reunification could take up to "three years." It seemed clear she was signaling that her 9-year-old daughter was not coming home. But the two DCP staff admitted the child wanted to be with her mother, and that mother and daughter had a special and loving bond. The younger case worker then said, "We just want to give her space to be a child for a while."

It was the most illogical and unfathomable statement I had ever heard.

It was on record that the young girl was mortified at having been removed from her mum, and that she appeared "grief stricken" at first visitation with her mother. The carer at the time noted the child sobbed at night. It was documented that the child's most loved person in the world was her mum; that there were nine or more affidavits testifying what an amazing and caring mother she was – plus the existing Family Court order ordered that the child "shall not be removed from the mother's care."

The removal of the child had disrupted her life so completely. The regular endearing picnic-dinners on the beach with mum ended; the regular after-school afternoons with a bunch of class friends coming over ended; camping holidays ended; her mother at sports days or at school play performances ended; hugs and kisses goodnight from mum ended. The child was completely and deliberately isolated from her loving mother. It must have been psychologically traumatizing and life-changing.

The mother, too, became isolated from society – including her extended family because she could not go where her child was. From being the hub of the family, she was soon excluded from family gatherings (e.g., Xmas, weddings, and holidays); and she was barred from the school (where she was previously a popular parent rep). By degrees all her friends (mainly mums from the same school) drifted on to continue life with their children. In the end, her only contact with children and past friends was when she was asked to babysit. She became a social leper -- totally isolated.

It is a process of what I call 'social purgatory'. These parents, while attempting to protect their children or challenge the government, are destroyed completely: psychologically, socially, financially and professionally. They become shadows of their former selves. The trauma acts upon their brains in well described, scientifically validated ways, so that they appear to be distraught and are looked on as unbalanced. Their testimonies can become easily disbelieved and discredited, so that the abusers and their enablers are made safe, while the children are lost to abuse or to the exploitation of the system. I believe department staffs know what they are doing to these distraught parents, and it is a deliberate strategy for control over them and their children. A 'broken' client is a client that is unable to challenge their actions. They must witness this dissolution and emotional disintegration over and over again. I have lost count of the times I have heard the 'same' story.

So, the case worker's comment, "We just want to give her space to be a child for a while" seemed grotesquely abhorrent. It was so contrary to the sum of my experiences living on four continents over 6 decades on this earth. The case worker seemed naïve and in training; but the supervisor, was an old hand. A path well-trodden! This was just another day at the office for them -- "business as usual." Nothing that was said or done had anything to do with the safety, or the emotional and physical well-being of this child. I defy any public servant, minister or judge to challenge me on this.

It was difficult to wrap my head around the insanity of their thinking. In my articles on Gumshoe News I have written that men are mainly the focus when it comes to pedophilia, but I also write that there is an army of women that enable pedophilia and facilitate the trauma, torture and psychological abuse of children. There is a part of me that feels sorry for these people who act so callously against children, as it may stem from their abuse or from "a profound emptiness" in their lives.

In April 2021 on Gumshoe News, Tony Ryan with ten years working in child protection and family welfare commented on social workers[25] being "emotionally estranged." He wrote that these public servants see kids "as expressions of ideology... an anti-parenting ideology." I'm sure there are many good people who go into social work to better the world. I apologize to these good people, as I don't hear what they are doing because I am not alerted to their positive actions. I'm only sent the worst cases. But I am wondering why these good welfare officers are not more vocal about the failures that they must surely be witness to. [Tonight I happened to meet a Victorian social worker. We had a brief discussion on the dirty tricks of the department, and she confirmed many concepts in this book. She said, "They don't want to fix things; they want dollars to expand services." I was pleased to hear she's planning to write her own book next year.]

I have also observed that some child protection staffs view parents challenging the system to get their children back a negative. A young couple wanting to get their baby back was faced with this comment by the Supervisor, "If you are confrontational, we'll push back." Their attempt to challenge the department in court was seen as "confrontational." It's a catch-22 -- without a challenge, they will probably never get their baby back. Another mum was told, "Just do what the department wants, then things will get better. You'll get more access."

What does the department want? They want control over your lives; they want your children on their books, and they want compliant subservient "clients."

Twisted Language

From all the horrific accounts I have heard, I do not believe – for a second – in the fuzzy language from the government's child departments, nor the wording of the law. These words bend the mind and disarm the reader. The government mantra is to keep children "safe." Wording on the government's DSS (Department of Social Services) site would warm anyone's heart:

> "Children and young people in Australia have the right to grow up safe, connected and supported in their family, community and culture. They have the right to grow up in an environment that enables them to reach their full potential."[26]

Sadly, this does not reflect (my) reality. I get an overwhelming feeling of nausea reading passages like this because my inbox is filled with accounts and cases of children being harmed by the actions of government departments and courts, and where they are forbidden connection to those they love. *Can you imagine that –* imposing brutal constraints to disconnect a child from the person/s they love?

Firstly, children in government care are in much more danger – four times more danger, in fact. You might direct me to websites where the government claims it cares about child protection, but the wording in their reports and mission statements is a facade disguising their actual intentions:

> "We work to support the safety and well-being of vulnerable children, young people and families. This work also supports the Premier's Priorities to protect our most vulnerable children, increase permanency for children in out-of-home care (OOHC), and reduce domestic and family violence reoffending.

The pleasingly positive and affirmative language (above) is taken from item 2.6 *Children and families thrive* in the New South Wales

FACS (the Department of Communities and Justice, DCJ) Annual Report 2019-2020.[27] To continue:

> "Protecting our most vulnerable children: During 2019–20, our caseworkers saw 35,241 [NSW] children and young people at risk of significant harm (ROSH). This was a 14 per cent increase from 2018–19...

> "Keeping families together where possible: [In] 2019–20, we worked …to support children to remain safely at home and to prevent them from entering OOHC."

I have already mentioned the overwhelming distortions of removing Aboriginal children, and that many of these removals across the country are done on accusations of "emotional abuse", but there are some encouraging actions providing 380 places to help keep families through Permanency Support Program (PSP).

It is clear that many children are removed AGAINST their will. I have photographs, videos, and accounts of children sobbing and screaming to not be ripped from their protective parent or parents. There's a video of young lad clawing at a window desperate to be with his mother. When he is picked up by the social worker to be taken away he screams blue murder and shouts at her, "I want my mummy. I hate you. Give me my mummy... (then hysterically) LEAVE ME ALONE." I have a recording of a young girl pleading with a Court Sheriff for half an hour to not be forced back to live with her abuser. The Sheriff apologized and said there's nothing he can do; that he had witnessed hundreds of similar family court cases (where the court defied the wishes of the children). Hundreds of cases in just one court!

The hand written notes by children; and the images, videos, and recordings are haunting. Most of these are discarded by the courts. So, please don't tell me that the mission to keep children 'safe' and 'connected' is working.

Understanding Child Abuse

Australians can be proud of many things. Australia is now ranked as the world's No.1 Test cricket team. I live, allegedly, in the world's most livable city, Melbourne, and I've ridden past an inland Taipan on the Birdsville track, the world's most venomous snake. But one statistic shrouds the country in deep shame. Australia is the gold medal winner in child sexual abuse, with "one significant study noting Australia as having the highest reported rate for child sexual abuse of girls internationally at 21.5%."[28]

To fully understand child trading and trafficking in Australia, one has to comprehend the statistics on child sexual abuse. There is a collective denial and this is partly due to the media, ignorance, apathy, and secrecy. After four years in communication with SAPOL, the ISS, and oversight bodies, I came to the conclusion that police PROTOCOL *is* to conceal child sexual abuse evidence – unless it is impossible to do so.

There are now ads on television encouraging the reporting of child sexual abuse, but history has demonstrated that when a parent reports sexual abuse to protect their child or children, a likely outcome is that they will lose their children. Beware!

The Office of the Children's Guardian (OCG), responsible for the administration of the NSW Working with Children Check, initiated the well-researched paper "Understanding the process of child sexual abuse disclosure: What does the research tell us?" by *Collin-Vézina, De La Sablonnière-Griffin, Palmer & Milne,* 2015 p.123. The study found that Australia was leading the world in child sexual abuse of girls (as above), but many people think this statistic of 21.5% is conservative.

The research revealed that as few as 8.3% of children disclosed sexual abuse in a formal (e.g. forensic) setting close to the occurrence of such abuse (*Priebe & Svedin,* 2008), and that many children don't disclose because they might be in a dependent relationship with their abuser. Those that did faced serious negative consequences.[29]

Possibly the most important statistic is about 'false reporting'. The research does not support an assertion that young children's disclosures are often false, and finds that false disclosures are repeatedly reported as rare as 1% - 1.5%. It's hard for a young child to lie about sexual abuses in a sophisticated and consistent manner.

This begs the question: why would the Family, Children's and Youth courts deem most children's disclosures as false? Judges and magistrates consistently ignore disclosures of rape and sexual abuse even if the children told numerous mandatory reporters. They often shame and blame the mother, for example, labelling her delusional or a coacher. In essence, these judicial officers are calling these children liars.

Imagine for a moment, for example, how courageous a sexually abused child has to be to tell a teacher, her doctor, her mother, her psychologist and then a stranger (a police officer) of horrific experiences that are shameful to her. She hopes she will be protected. But, the opposite happens. The system and the court often punish the child.

- In the Family Court it is very likely the child will be ordered into the custody of his or her abuser, and the protective parent might only have contact under strict supervision – if at all.

- In a state Children's Court, it is highly likely the child will be appropriated from the care of the protective parent and be placed into state care. In many instances, the child will be vulnerable to abuse and rape whilst in care.

ALECOMM's (Australian Legislative Ethics Commission) response to the ALRC's Inquiry into Family Law Courts, confirmed there is an ingrained culture in managing child sexual abuse by covering it up. ALECOMM's 2018 report suggested the need for a Royal Commission -- demonstrating that court decisions ESCALATE RISK for children.[30] In the majority of cases, the child was labelled a liar; with judges disregarding substantiations of child abuse by protection agencies and police, and protective-parents being labelled delusional or psychotic, coachers or emotional abusers.

So-called Independent Children's Lawyers and Family Court Experts (testifying as the 'Court Reporters') often encouraged the courts to send children who had disclosed sexual abuse back to live with their abuser and that contact with the protective-parent cease. It is quite difficult to read these reports as they as horrifying, so it's clear these Experts hold little regard for the well-being, safety or 'best interests' of the child.

This was confirmed in my 2018 GumshoeNews.com (Family Court) survey[31] Question 7 asked [71 responses]: *"Who DID believe your child when she or he disclosed sexual abuse? From the categories below identify someone (even one person) who believed your child?* :

- Members of my family (58)
- Your psychologist/psychiatrist (41)
- A doctor, nurse, medical personnel (29)
- Anyone in the police, detective etc., (21)
- Other persons (20)
- Child Protective Service Officers (15)
- Social workers, supervised visit personnel (12)
- Court appointed experts (6)
- Court appointed psychiatrist (3)
- ICL, independent child lawyer (2)
- The judge; the court (2)

In the survey, those charged with protecting the children and ensuring their rights were shown to be the most likely persons to discount the child's disclosures and their experiences. This does not align with the science where false disclosures are repeatedly reported as rare as 1% - 1.5%.[32]

What is most revealing in all of this is the deliberate spoliation of evidence. Spoliation of evidence is the intentional, reckless, or negligent withholding, hiding, altering, fabricating, or destroying of evidence relevant to a legal proceeding. And in many cases relevant to the protection of the child. This happens all the time, and in my survey (Q19) about 56% of the responders claimed evidence was destroyed. Preserving evidence is an ancient and well-documented common law principle inferring that when a party destroys a document, the court may presume that the document would have been detrimental to their case. The Latin phrase *Contra Spoliaterem Omnia Praesumuntur* refers to the consequences of document destruction, and that "all things are presumed against the despoiler." So why would a Family or Children's Court judge order evidence of sexual abuse to be destroyed? Is the court intent on hiding sexual abuse? Shockingly, in Q21 I asked: *"Did the Judge destroy evidence, or order that evidence be destroyed?"* Of 55 responders, 17 (30.91%) said YES.

Surely a judge ordering a parent to destroy evidence of sexual abuse (without testing the evidence) is potentially placing that child back in harm's way? I hope you begin to see how irrational the protection and court system is. There is a deliberate apparatus to suppress child sexual abuse in this country – and it goes all the way to the top. Even though 8,000 victims were heard in the *Royal Commission into Institutional Responses to Child Sexual Abuse*, tens of thousands of victims were not heard as they fell outside the commission's remit. An ABC article noted "…up to 80 per cent of all child sexual abuse occurs within a familial relationship, not an institution like a church or a school." Attempts to have the Family Court of Australia included in the Royal Commission failed.

It is obvious that some children need to be kept safe from a damaged or dangerous home, but with nearly 50,000 children (1-

18) in OOHC; the numbers of these children that fall into this serious at-risk category is unknown. The reality – and cruel irony -- is that children taken from loving homes suffer psychological abuse through separation. Statistics from ALECOMM[33] and other government data state that the 1% of children in government care are 20X more likely to die than those children at home; and about 4 to 6 times more likely to be sexually abused. And these children, when they have children, are more likely become future clients of the so-called protection services.

Nothing makes sense in the business of child protection. On the one hand you have judges discounting the child's disclosures and ordering evidence be destroyed, and on the other hand the Commissioner for Children and Young People claiming "Victorian authorities failed to protect the most vulnerable children from sexual predators… after an Ombudsman investigation found the state had one of the country's weakest systems to screen adults who work with children." (The Age 14 September 2022 article, entitled "State's most vulnerable children 'failed by authorities'."[34])

Advocates report the system as having "systemic failures", or being in "crisis". I think the so-called failures are a cover – a veil to allow a child trafficking-type system to operate with impunity. I believe, the 'protection' system was designed to operate as it does like a well-oiled machine that permeates a perverted cultural belief that the child "remove-and-place" program is the solution.

The science demonstrates that taking children unwillingly from their biological mother (or father) – based on innuendo and hearsay -- is tantamount to TORTURE. The outcome is a system that dispatches both mother or father and child to a disrupted life of social impoverishment.

It's a bloody social disaster.

Imagine your torment if police *planted* evidence and you were then falsely accused of murdering someone, resulting in you being given a life sentence!

Now...

Imagine your torment if police *concealed* evidence so that you were falsely accused of suspected emotional abuse of your child, and your child was taken from you – bestowing you with a broken family and a life sentence of separation!

Imagine if you found out after surviving 18 years in numerous foster homes that your life was stolen from you and that your deeply caring and loving parents were falsely accused of harming you when they took you to a hospital for a checkup!

Deliberate Intent to Harm

In the previous chapter I discussed how bad decisions lead to bad outcomes. It might be difficult to grasp the absurdity or the intended evil of such conduct: removing the child from the custody and care of their protective parent, and for that child to be then made available to the abuser (and/or the wider pedophile community). I believe these are carefully planned and deliberate actions AGAINST the 'best interests' or safety of the child, and I will describe one such malevolent insanity.

In the case of young Ella, her mother Joanne had 'won' in family court and was awarded sole custody. As I previously described, six weeks later Ella was (physically) injured when at her father's. This was reported, but it led to her being removed from her mother's care in 2018 (because Officer Thompson had concealed the police interview where the child had described in detail how her father had in the past sexually and physically abused her). After her child was removed, Joanne was unaware that the St Mary's DCP team was secretly working towards reunifying Ella with her father -- to award him custody. I believe the entire matter was an orchestrated plan to switch custody via the "back door" in a State court (in violation of the Federal Court order). The DCP's reunification with the father had, however, struck a hurdle as Ella remained defiant in her resistance; and this without her mother's support (as she saw her mum only one hour a week under strict supervision). But the St Mary's DCP team forged ahead determined to keep Ella from her mother (who she desperately wanted to be with) and place her with her father (whom she was most fearful of, and had claimed was her abuser). I have rarely come across such resilience and fortitude in a child. Even after a year of separation from her mum, Ella refused to retract her allegations; even though a DCP-approved psychologist was court-ordered to assist Ella in therapy to change her thinking and make her believe that she had never been abused. (Is this a form of court-ordered grooming and brainwashing? I would say so!)

But that's only where the insanity begins. It was in mid-2019 that Joanne managed to subpoena the (concealed) police interview and watch it. It was shocking for her. For over an hour long her then 8-year-old detailed, in the most innocent language, being tied up; forced to drink yukky yellowy white stuff; having knives in her bottom; being put against the wall and her pants pulled down, and a 'private part' pushed in her mouth.

Joanne called the case worker and the St Mary's team leader, Ms Wood. But Ms Wood would have nothing of it and refused to watch the video of the police interview. (It took a year for the court to order her to watch it.) Now cognizant of the serious allegations in the police interview, Ms Wood and her team ignored these and forged ahead with reunification with the father anyway. They also ignored more than a dozen other reports in the system, plus the 2016 substantiation by a CPS investigator and Families SA. It is difficult to fathom the sheer lunacy of their actions. They had several hearings in "Reunification Court" – a side show of the Youth Court Star Chamber – deliberately excluding Joanne. They were RECKLESSLY INTENT on placing the child in harm's way; with the person who she repeatedly and consistently identified as the person who had sexually abused her. These actions (of defying the child) were deemed acceptable by the Youth Court and *everyone* in the department (and some family). It seems not one person couched caution (s31) (1) of the *Children and Young People (Safety) Act* 2017--"if a person suspects on reasonable grounds that a child or young person is, or may be, at risk of harm... they must report that suspicion..." . My vote is that those responsible should be charged for Criminal Negligence (s14) 1(d) of the *Criminal Law Consolidation Act*... i.e., a person acts unlawfully when they "fail to take steps that he or she could reasonably be expected to have taken in the circumstances to protect the victim from harm..."

In the end, the child saved herself, and the DCP abandoned reunification – but they remained at war with the mother.

Unimaginable Suffering

After answering many desperate calls, and being with parents who have lost children to the government, I can now say that having a child ripped from your care by "authorities", for many, is a living death experience. It is possibly the worst thing you can do to a human. And for as long as it lasts, that parent is dying a death – every single day -- and is granted no relief.

Do you remember the scene in the film *Sophie's Choice* when the Nazi officer at the concentration camp forces a mother (played by Meryl Streep) to decide which child she is going to 'sacrifice' (give up)? She decides, and as they drag her daughter away you are witness to the blood curdling cries of despair.

Those cries happen every day – many times every day – in Star Chamber courts and in department "visitation" centres across this country. I have witnessed mothers implode with grief before me or on the phone. I was having coffee with one such mother the other day when a baby on a far table started babbling. It took only seconds for this mum to break down sobbing. It is like watching their hearts being excised from their bodies. And it is torture witnessing these people being tortured day after day, month after month, and year after year. I'm sure they would be willing to be flogged to near-death in public if they could keep their offspring. Many say life is not worth living without the children.

I am in regular contact with one mum (I'll call her N) who had three children removed on the most spurious, malicious and untested claims. I thank her for giving me further insight in writing this chapter. I know her life story in some detail, and she is a survivor of a brutal rape experience. When she was being choked and raped, she thought she was going to die, but she says that experience was a passing one, and was minor in comparison to the torment and agony she feels each and every day after her children were removed by the department.

On the evening television news we have witnessed a mother pleading to the public to find her lost child. Millions feel empathy and compassion. Her emotional distress and her crying, and pleading through uncontrollable sobs is seen as acceptable – no, we expect this type of reaction from a distressed parent. But when a mother loses her children to the government, firstly, she is forbidden to go public. Secondly, if she shows her distress, sobs and cries out, this is used against her. "Your Honour, the mother's outbursts of emotion distressed her children, and she is unable to remain calm. We have assessed her as unstable." If you show a natural emotion, the department will use this against you.

The mum on television may be distraught as she doesn't know where her child is, but with the other mum *does* know where her children are but is unable to protect them. It could be said that this makes a mother's living experience infinitely worse. This mother has the knowledge that her children have either, been ordered back into the custody of a sexual abuser (as per the children's allegations), or they are destined to the love-less world of foster care – where they are (statistically) in more danger. This applies to both mum and dad. I have been in contact with a grandmother and father, where he had medical proof that his drug addicted and mentally unstable ex-partner had damaged his son's neck. It must have been torment. Years of trying to get authorities or the courts to intervene and protect the child failed.

It is a parent's instincts to protect. It is in our DNA. So can you imagine the torment of isolation and despair when they are forbidden contact and are no longer able to protect or nurture their children. It would go against every natural instinct. An Aboriginal person will tell you, "In my mob, family is core. Without family you become lost." It is not surprising that when the government removes Aboriginal children from family, this creates a wave of destruction. They have and still are destroying First Nations by destroying the family bonds.

And these removals are often imposed on the basis of hearsay, innuendo, or a bought and/or fabricated opinion. I have to think that those imposing these sentences (orders) don't have the emotional intelligence or capacity to comprehend what they have done, rather than being nourished by power, money and maliciousness. The torture of the parent also never ends (unless they end it themselves in suicide). I'll describe some of what N has gone through. She describes how she watched her three children deteriorate under government care, and

> "If I complained or questioned the social workers, they would threaten me in some way. They would intimidate me by warnings of 'We're going to cancel visitation'. I knew they were doing badly, had not been properly cared for, but I couldn't challenge them. I was forced to participate in their lie that the separation was good for the children, when I knew it was terrible."

N continues,

> "Each week, for that one precious hour, you can see what is happening to them. When you see them with bruises, you are not allowed to ask them how they got hurt; when you see your child sad, they don't want you to ask why. When you hear your child screaming as the case worker drags them away after the one hour visitation it becomes your fault."

I've heard the conversations with N described by many grief-stricken parents. Joanne was at one point forbidden to give her daughter notes and cards that said "I love you so much". Parents are discouraged to show photographs of their former happy family days, as "It might give the children false hope that they are going home." Hope of reunification is stamped out ruthlessly.

Mother N describes how,

> "I had to just watch as the kidnappers hurt my children. But I had to remain calm and composed. I remember one day my

disabled son was so desperate not to leave me, and was fighting for his life to not be pushed into the car. He was most definitely hurt by being so forcibly shoved, like a concertina, into the back seat. I started filming with my phone. The case worker slammed the car door closed, then turned to me: 'I'm going to report you for what you've done.' She did report me. I was blamed for the children's distress at leaving me. They'd say, 'You're disrupting the departure, encouraging the children to rebel.' And then they told me, 'Bring a bag of treats. And you can give it to them to distract them when you leave so they don't get upset.' They accused me of upsetting my children for saying 'I miss you... I love you so much.' Every action I took, even if it is to remind them I was their mother, was viewed negatively. I was always blamed for any distress, when it was all due to their trauma of being separated from their mother."

She tells me, and so has Joanne, that there is only one thing worse than seeing the grief of their children when visitation ends — i.e., when the children are crying desperately wanting their mother's safety and love — is when they don't. N describes how her children's attitude changed after 9 months.

"What is worse is when the fight for more cuddles stops. They no longer fight to be with you, and they come to accept the chains of guardianship and the restrictions. They no longer cried or hung on as the department had broken their spirit, and they became hollow and numb at departure. That's the most terrible feeling, like I have betrayed them."

The unimaginable suffering is emotional pain, but this is also making people unwell — very unwell. It is in every cell of their body. The advocates and supporters of these parents have to protect themselves too, because even listening to these horror stories is debilitating in every way (so thank you for reading).

A Note on the Family Court

I have discussed the "remove-and-place" program by the Out-of-Home Care multi-billion dollar enterprise and I detail the 'rort' on the tax-payer in a later chapter. I believe the whole idea of "removals" should be interrogated anyway. The Family Court, on the other hand, is a federal jurisdiction with the intention of dealing with custody disputes – and it's a twist on the financially lucrative "remove-and-place" programs. This is a court where citizens pay large sums of money for the privilege of having a judge decide on which parent to remove from, and where to place the merchandise (i.e., their children).

It is also well established that the Family Courts are unable to handle cases involving child sexual abuse. The default is for the court and ICL (child's lawyer) to disbelieve the child – a fact that was revealed in my 2018 Gumshoe survey, and by many other people. This usually results in the protective parent being accused of being an emotional abuser (without evidence); or suffering from a mental disorder, or of PAS (Parent Alienation Syndrome). Inevitably, the judge then orders custody of the child to his or her alleged abuser. This happens over and over again.

Family Court is like a Financial Osmosis Operating System – the more conflict generated, the more money is drawn into the scheme. Children are part of us, so no expense is spared. In my 2018 Gumshoe survey, I asked this question (Q15): *How much MONEY have you lost (or spent) trying to achieve (or manage) your outcome in the family court, so far?* 71 people answered the question. The responses were astonishing. 39% of people said less than $50,000; 22.54% said $51,000 – 150,000, and 22.54% between $151,000 – 350,000; and just under 6% said they expended more than $750,000. Wow! And this is only from one side. It means 32 people of the 71 paid out between $50,000 to 350,000 and all of them said they lost almost everything dear to them (i.e., their kids).

What a money-guzzling system! Imagine paying big money to solve a dispute with a system that encourages more accusations and conflict to solve the initial dispute? It's an adversarial system and there's always going to be a loser, and it's clear that the good liars and psycho or sociopaths fared better in court.

I recently watched an alternative media outlet interviewing a family court lawyer who said the court is rigged against men. It was a very gender-divisive piece. Depending on who you speak to, there will be thousands of men and thousands of women who feel the Family Court is rigged. Correct, yes, it's a rigged system; rigged AGAINST parents -- both fathers and mothers, depending on the case – and the system doesn't care about the children. Many say the court intentionally makes the wrong decision, and in his famous speech, Senator Bill Heffernan explained how children are used as "tools".

Obviously you can be forced to court if your ex is socially dysfunctional – and both genders play a part in this. But how demoralizing is it that people subscribe to an adversarial system that will forever control your time with your offspring. A custody-control order will then dictate the time, place, and days for years to come on the relationship with your beloved children. How disempowering! And, those ICLs that advocated for, and the judges that wrote the order don't give one single iota about you, your ex or your children. It's just business as usual in the Family Court Industrial Complex.

I know several parents, who have been subjected to years of emotional abuse from a partner, and then the court (and judge) takes over the gas lighting – and their orders facilitate coercive control over the protective parent and the children.

Imagine if the system were changed from adversarial to amiable, cooperative and child-conducive – and sorted in a nurturing environment for the children? *Dream on?*

PART THREE

Complaining is a hopeless exercise – it's a journey to nowhere. There is a firewall protecting public officials.

"The very word secrecy is repugnant in a free and open society." --*John F. Kennedy*

Pass the Parcel

I spent four years trying to get the South Australian authorities to investigate the malfeasance and misfeasance of public servants. I wrote hundreds of letters and made over two hundred phone calls. It was a hopeless endeavour that led down a cul-de-sac every time.

It was, and is, an endless game of "pass the parcel" -- and the music never stops. The Child Protection Minister might direct me to the department's complaint office or the Attorney-general; the Ombudsman might direct me to the Office of Public Integrity (OPI); the Independent Commission Against Corruption SA (ICAC) to IIS (Internal Investigation Services of SAPOL), and IIS might refer me back to the department (DCP); the Prime Minister to the Human Rights Commissioner, and the Judicial Conduct Commissioner (JCC) might advise me to get legal representation, etc. All protective parents are very familiar with this treadmill. It's a washing machine of communication garbage.

In many letters I outlined the facts of a child's terrible sexual abuse allegations; notifications by mandatory reporters; details of crimes concealing evidence, and how this led to the girl's unlawful removal from her protective mother. I pointed out that despite all these reports, the DCP was attempting to reunify the child with her alleged abuser (an action that was criminally negligent).

As I have said, not a single person or leader wanted to put their hand up. I correct myself; just before Xmas in 2018, one woman, Emily Strickland the deputy Ombudsman, did believe me and sounded horrified on our long phone call. She promised to put her best investigator on the case in the New Year. But in 2019 my communication with her was impeded. Things had changed; her engagement changed. She was later moved sideways from the Ombudsman's office to another portfolio.

It became clear that the Ombudsman, SAPOL's IIS, and the corruption oversight bodies (ICAC, OPI, JCC, etc.) would never investigate this matter. There was always a lame excuse. The state is just averse in investigating the misfeasance and corruption of their public servants.

Well, you can't expect the fox to investigate the hen house.

A typical response was, for example, "the actions [i.e., concealing child rape disclosures and making false notes] of the police officer did not warrant any disciplinary action" (a letter by Detective Chief Inspector Sharman APM). Astonishingly, the replies from the South Australian government, specifically from the Minister for Child Protection, usually ended with this paragraph:

> "If you or any other person is aware of a person or child in immediate danger contact the SA police on 000. Alternatively, to report a reasonable suspicion that a child is being abused or neglected phone the Child Abuse Report Line (CARL) 13 14 87."

What! It is a gob-smacking and obscene betrayal of the child. After presenting evidence and facts of abuse, rape, assault and torture (over a dozen reports over 3 to 4 years), police transcripts, actual photographs of the injuries, the minister's reply was "if you have reasonable suspicion…[of abuse]" report it, but, in essence saying, 'however, we're taking no action of the factual evidence you supplied'. Nothing was ever done. Nothing will be done.

And they *never* ever mentioned or seemed concerned about the plight of the child (e.g., what about considering a welfare check?).

The entire system is a sham.

You may ask, "Is that why people say the country might be run by a pedophile cult?" Yes, and I believe SAPOL's protocol (i.e., the South Australian Police) is to conceal abuse unless it is impossible to do so. I challenged them on this, and it was never denied.

A few replies from authorities suggested that my letter raised issues that are difficult and may bring up strong feelings for *me*, and advised that I might wish to seek Lifeline's services (13 11 14).

Yes, they are issues for me, but this was to deflect my complaint – and again, there was never a mention of the child or what difficulties she might be going through.

What are these people being paid to do?

To those leaders reading this book that do and say nothing – you are the sugar that quickens this cancer in society. To say nothing is to propagate the suffering. To those judges that discard the wishes of a child, you are the encephalopathy to society – the brain dysfunction.

I imagine some leading public servants and ministers have minimal participation in their portfolio as their hands appear to be tied – either by fear or forced complicity. Or maybe they just don't give a damn -- or as some suggest: they do know what's going on and are complicit in the child protection racket. Claude-Frédéric Bastiat, 1801-1850 (economist, writer and Member of the French National Assembly) allegedly said,

> "When plunder becomes a way of life for a group … in a society, over the course of time they create for themselves a legal system that authorizes it and a moral code that glorifies it."

This is a very apt quote for 2023 where the 'plunder' of children in a so-called righteous legal system has become acceptable, even exalted. I have often said if our government officials and leaders, especially the ministers for child protection -- are disinterested in assisting Australia's most vulnerable (e.g., protecting a child that has disclosed versions of rape) does it mean they are not governing *for* the people?

Welcome to Australia, the land of the fair go. *Sure!*

In 2023, after talking to a young man in the Commonwealth Ombudsman's office, I decided to produce a report for the Australian Federal Police (AFP) -- as the AFP has the primary law enforcement responsibility for investigating corruption and fraud upon the Commonwealth through the misappropriation of funds.[35] This includes unlawful use of material or services, causing a loss, misuse of Commonwealth assets, and cartel conduct, etc., plus any conspiracy to defeat the course of Justice. I decided to produce a report – for investigation – to the AFP (Australian Federal Police).

My Notification of Trafficking

The States have the jurisdiction to investigate abduction (which they will never do if they are the abductors), whereas the Commonwealth is burdened with investigating child human trafficking. I contend these may be individual cases of abduction, per se, but there is an apparatus – a government cartel operating in tandem with the court set up to remove children from their homes. These children are then trafficked into "care" facilitating the Out-of-Home-Care (OOHC) Industrial Complex to thrive – thrive on the purse of the tax-payer and ever increasing child protection budgets.

As described on the AFP website[36], "Human trafficking is the physical movement of people across and within borders through deceptive means, force or coercion. The people who commit human trafficking offences are motivated by the continuing exploitation of their victims..." This would imply that the wrongful or unlawful removal of children for financial gain in Australia is trafficking.

Again, let me emphasize. I am not talking about children who need to be brought into care; I am specifically referring to the cases of children being wrongfully or unlawfully removed. I conservatively estimate that of the approximately 50,000 children (1-18) in OOHC, at least 20,000 should never have been removed. Others estimate this to be higher. Remember that only 25,000 children were dispatched over 80 years from their parents in the UK and sent Down Under – allegedly as punishment; just like Ella was for speaking out to her teacher.

Whatever we call this business (e.g., The Child Removal Industrial Complex -- CRIC) it has become a significant part of the Australian economy.

My report to the AFP noted three (Commonwealth) crimes:

- Conspiracy to Defeat the Course of Justice through the Children's Courts – *Crimes Act 1914* s42 (3) (b) … intended to obstruct, prevent, pervert or defeat the course of justice.[37]

- Fraud and Corruption upon the Commonwealth, and Misappropriation of funds.[38] The Commonwealth Fraud Control Policy defines fraud as 'dishonestly obtaining a benefit, or causing a loss, by deception or other means'. [39]

- Child trafficking – the wrongful or deceptive removal and exploitation of children for financial gain.[40]

I decided to submit my report to the AFP, and received an email instructing me to submit the document at their offices in Little Lonsdale Street, Melbourne. I followed someone into the building as the doors opened. Mistake! It alerted an armed response as public entry is forbidden. Two pleasant armed officers came outside to inform me that any report must be emailed, which I did, to the Exploitation of Children in Australia (25 April 2023) to NOSSC (National Operations State Service Centre). (As of the time of writing: 1/10/2023, I have received no response.)

My report to the AFP report (#132282) details how certain government agencies, public servants and outside contractors are using the Children and Youth courts via secretive and deceptive practices, under the guise of child protection, to unwarrantedly and unlawfully 'traffic' children. I noted, as have many others, that these children's courts are nothing more than 'star chambers.' They appear subservient to the objectives of the "Cash-for-Kids business", and 'rubber stamp' decisions daily.

Intrinsic incentives come from within – whereas extrinsic incentives involve a material reward, like money or a job (or coercion, or cultural norms). Monetary reward feeds into the psychology of behavioural economics – i.e., the more children removed into OOHC, the larger become the state budgets. Plus, the flow of funds stimulates jobs and growth -- seemingly benefitting a broader segment of the population. Over several decades of servicing the OOHC industry it has become a billion dollar enterprise. Many people's livelihoods depend on children being so-called protected -- i.e., removed -- and the persons benefitting range from social workers, agency executives, psychologists, psychiatrists, foster care placement agencies, carers, medical professionals, crown solicitors and barristers, children lawyers, magistrates and judges. If parents challenge the government, then more people become involved (e.g., professionals, teams of lawyers, etc.,) to compete against the parents.

Are there individual or organizational bonus-type payments acting as incentives to remove children, whether warranted on not? Pastor Paul believes so and has some evidence about this. Even judges are not immune to the seduction of money. In what came to be known as the 'kids-for-cash scandal', two juvenile court judges in the US, Mark Ciavarella and Michael Conahan, orchestrated a (zero-tolerance policy) scheme to send children to for-profit jails in exchange for kickbacks of $2.8 million. A district court Judge awarded US$106 million in compensatory damages and US$100 million in punitive damages to nearly 300 people.

Though some people may do good work, many benefit financially from the trafficking of children from safe homes. Their mortgage payments depend on it, and many new recruits fall in line with the toxic culture of 'removals' as the desired and default outcome. These public servants know the extraction tricks and believe they are immune to prosecution. They are! Many abuse the law and use the power of the protection agencies to camouflage any of their deceptive or fraudulent action.

These criminal actions against loved and well-cared for children and their loving and competent parents is simply unacceptable. It's a fraud on the commonwealth tax payer and a crime against humanity. And as the industry expands it erodes the fundamental principal of humanity's existence – family. It disrupts the social and emotional collective intelligence of our society.

"Children are our most valuable resource." --
31st President of the United States,

--Herbert Hoover

"Our children are our greatest treasure. They are our future. Those who abuse them tear at the fabric of our society and weaken our nation."

— *Nelson Mandela*

The Trade -- Figuring Out Exploitation

The term "child trafficking" conjures up images of African children between the ages of 8 and 14 being trucked across a border to work in the Côte d'Ivoire (Ivory Coast)[41] cocoa plantations.[42] The worth of each child could be determined by their labour-output which might be valued at A\$5 to 8/day – these earnings derived from the sale of cocoa. Let's say a trafficked child might be "valued" around A\$2,500 each year to the 'syndicate', so trading (trafficking) 20,000 African children into labour could generate up to A\$50 plus million each year.

I suggest a more profitable option of trafficking children is through a sophisticated "remove-and-place" government program. There is no complex sale of merchandise (e.g., cacao), as the children *are* the merchandise. The income is sourced and derived from the tax-payer. And, ingeniously, there is no limiting factor for the industry -- as the more children in the program; the bigger are the budgets awarded. To get allocated more tax dollars, just some bewailing in parliament will suffice -- on the pretense of keeping children safe. It's a bloody brilliant business model (with the added bonus of making some of these children available to the wider pedophile community, like the good 'ol institution days).

Each child brought into the system becomes an asset (a "financial unit" as they termed in some State financial books) and the budgets, in general terms, roughly equates to \$60,000 - \$150,000 per child in care annually. Special needs children are said to 'cost' (in services) up to \$350 - 450,000 annually (or much more); this, in part, supported by the NDIS (National Disability Insurance Scheme). Annual costs for Residential care ranges from \$450,000 to 880,000[43]. Snatch a baby, and its future worth (an asset to the government's services business) is millions of dollars.

Considering the Ivory Coast example, compare this to my suggested value of the unwarranted "removing-and-placing" of 20,000 children in OOHC in Australia. It could contribute as much as \$2 plus Billion towards the Oz economy.

"The only thing necessary for the triumph of evil
is for good men to do nothing."

-- *Edmund Burke*

"Jobs and Growth"

Any Australian voter is familiar with this government mantra. In 2007, the number of children in OOHC was 5.8 to 1,000 children. This has now risen to over 8 per 1,000.[44]

A government report[45] stated that in 2010 there were 37 social workers for every 100,000 of the population. By 2020 it was 67 social workers per 100,000 – an 81% increase over that decade; with females making up 80% of this workforce. Over this same decade nursing dropped. And in 2020, 588,475 people were employed in community service industries (e.g., welfare, and child care services industry).

The Family Matters report, released by Secretariat of National Aboriginal and Islander Child Care (SNAICC), found 21,523 Indigenous children were in OOHC as of June 30, 2020. This truly shocking statistic represents that one in every 15.6 First Nations children living in Australia[46] was removed from home. That means 64 out of every 1,000 Indigenous children are in OOHC. And no one is listening to their *voice*. (It may not be strictly comparable, but UNICEF data estimates only 1 child per 1,000 is in residential care worldwide.[47])

It's become obvious that the more children under State guardianship; the more jobs are created – and the more tax is required to deliver ever-increasing services, salaries, fees, and profits. My *estimate* is for every one child removed, you are probably creating fours jobs across the entire welfare, medical and legal sectors associated with child 'removals'. And many of these children are extracted (through accusations of hearsay or opinion) on the basis of "emotional abuse" – an allegation that is legally ambiguous and problematic.

Is this multi-billion industry just about "Jobs and growth"?

Like Say's Law, the economist, J.B. Say, says, the core driver of markets is around employment, "Supply creates its own demand" and children are the product.

As an addendum to this chapter, there is another aspect to 'children are a resource' and the control of the State over your children. Charles McGavin, in his *brokensystemproductions.com* writes about the Nanny State[48]. In a survey he conducted in 2018, he found that of the parents whose children had been forcibly removed, a staggering 95%, were partially or fully reliant on Centrelink payments (This of course is for many reasons, and often due to one parent escaping domestic violence). He suggests that your children are not yours in the way that you might think. He writes:

"In order to understand how children in Australia are parented, and how they can be removed from their natural parents and placed with other carers, it is necessary to understand how the Australian system is structured. We rely heavily on a social security system. Many of the services that are provided for families are provided by the state, whether directly, or through contract to private agencies. The state has a huge involvement in the lives of all Australians.

"You virtually have no choice but to use services that are paid for by the state, and when the state pays they have a vested interest in your life as well as that of your children...

"When you give birth, you do so believing that your child is yours and you have autonomy over the way he or she is raised. To an extent this is correct; however it is governed by the Family Law Act 1975 which focuses on the rights of the child, and the responsibilities of the parent. A parent has no rights in regard to their children, except to raise them according to their culture... "

Fostering the Money Train

Approximately 81% of taxes in Australia are derived from Commonwealth tax-payers[49], and state governments receive funds proportionally to manage the large budgets of agencies and services that supposedly keep children safe – and in many instances, by removing them. This tax payer's money also supports those benefitting financially from unlawful removals, which is a deceit and a fraud on the taxpayer.

One has to wonder why so many former foster children, now adults, describe how they were moved from one foster home to the next until they finally exited the system. Was this because there's a broker's fee every time a child is moved to a new foster home? I have been told the fee is more under an emergency removal and could be as much as $30,000. That would be an incentive, would it not?

Foster parents have a meaningful participation in society. I know of twins who were sent to a wonderful foster home after their parents were killed (I think) in an accident. But on the other hand, I have heard of the most horrific accounts. Good foster parents have described how the department removed their foster child or children under the most extraordinary and disgraceful circumstances -- and how the children were greatly harmed, confused and humiliated by removing them from caring foster homes. I detail this in a chapter called the *Garbage Bag Children*.

A foster mum called me a few years ago. She had had three young foster siblings in her care for a few years. The relatives of the three children were very supportive of the foster placement, but without warning there was an emergency removal. I was told that the three young kids fought so hard and fiercely to not be removed, that the one little boy was sent to a clinic for his injuries. The three very young children were taken to another placement, but they kicked up such a fuss – wanting to return – that they were medically drugged to subdue them. Regardless, they still fought, desperate to return to the home they knew and where they felt loved. Eventually, to *break* the children so as to manage them, the three siblings were separated. The foster mum was broken, too. She feared she would lose her home if she challenged the department. She was confused as to why the children were removed from her care until one of the social workers whispered to her, privately. This is what I recall the foster mum saying she was told: "You showed them love. They were becoming attached. You can't show love, just give them what they need." I still wonder what happened to those children. It would be a miracle if they were together, but I doubt it.

Many mechanisms are in place to facilitate unwarranted removals from vulnerable or struggling parents. A vulnerable single mother might lose her baby at a birthing hospital with department claims of abnormal blood samples. I was emailed the other day with this message, "My friend is a midwife and she told me they have to report people to CPS simply for not presenting to a doctor before 13 weeks when pregnant!" Parents can lose all their child because one child has a medical condition which the department claims is from abuse or neglect. To be clear, I am referring to cases where deceit and/or malfeasance can easily be demonstrated. As I have already written, there is a culture to conceal child sexual abuse evidence unless impossible to do so. So, when a protective parent reports sexual abuse this can lead to them losing his or her children to the State.

I have lost count how many times I have spoken to a protective and caring working mother who has lost her children – and she says something like this: "Why did they take my kids? There's a drug addicted couple on Centrelink living next door with their four feral kids. They're dirty and neglected and the cops are called sometimes 'cause the parents are fighting and screaming. So why do these f'd-up parents have their kids, and I don't… when I'm a good mum." I have no answer.

These unwarranted removals make little sense – until one considers these children are just merchandise to an Industrial Complex benefitting financially from the "remove-and-place" programs – i.e., trading of kids. Profits and salaries are justified and enhanced by expanding "traffic" in product, and many are on big salaries. The Chief Executive of the DCP (SA), Cathy Taylor, was on close to $800,000 per annum.

I'm sure many involved are unaware of the true nature of the business model and just participate to make a living. No one wants to upset the lucrative gravy train. It's a sobering thought that removing a healthy newborn into permanent guardianship means the liability of care of approximate $80 – 180,000 a year, each year, for 18 years. If the child is 'special needs'; a significant disability, then the child's value could be as much as $400,000 to 600,000 in services each year. This is all funded by the taxpayer with the foster carers only getting a small portion. I'm sure most foster parents believe they are contributing to society with many making a sacrifice by offering their parental support to children in genuine need of care. However, I'm sure many are oblivious of the true nature of the 'racket'.

Many child advocates can name a number of psychiatrists who have made a career and a lot of money on maliciously advocating for the removal of children from good protective parents. It will ring a 'Bell' to those approximately 2,000 parents who have suffered reports of the most disastrous and unscientific nature from just one psychiatrist who cheerfully boasted his achievements on ABC radio.[50]

When protective family members challenge these unlawful removals in the courts they expend their life savings to save their children or grandchildren from abusive placements. If they are challenging the State, then there are further financial gains for the Crown's legal team, the children's legal team, court report writers, magistrates, and judges -- all benefiting from the Attorney-general's budget. The matter can drag on for years and the wheels of injustice churn slowly through hearings, trials and appeals. And when criminal actions by public servants are condoned, concealed or overlooked, this constitutes a further fraud on the Commonwealth.

Below, a diagram portraying the flow of children to support the flow of money:

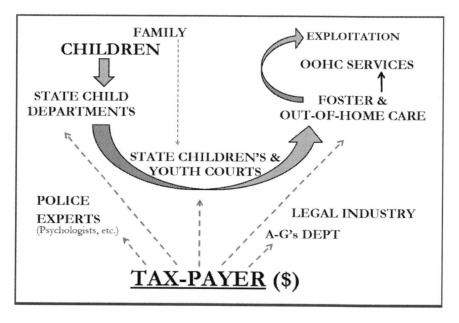

In the next chapter, I estimate the misappropriation of funds in just one case – that of mother Joanne and daughter Ella. I know every detail and have postulated that the wrongful removal of Ella generated at least $1,725,000 over five years to salaries, fees, etc. I have been conservative, and it could well be in the region of $3 to 4 million.

This all could have been prevented had just one ... just ONE public servant spoken out and did the right thing.

Nuts and Bolts of the Rort

Let me be clear in my explanation of the misappropriation of funds in the case of Joanne and her daughter, Ella (not their real names) that the facts undisputedly demonstrate that the claim against the mother was a deceit. Every dollar expended by the State after May 2018, after the child was removed, was used to defraud the court.

Let's begin the case study: A police interview with the child by Officer Chloe Thompson was conducted in November 2017 where the child disclosed versions of rape, torture, being tied up and physically abused (by her father). It is extremely disturbing to watch. A veteran in this field from the US with 38 years of experience testified in court in support of every word of the child.

Thompson had fabricated her police notes of the interview, denigrating Ella's entire testimony, by writing something the child did NOT say (e.g., "I forgot what I'm supposed to say"). This fabricated sentence implied the child was coached by someone. It was a lie. She then unlawfully concealed these crucial allegations from the Family Court; from CARL (Child Abuse Report Line), from CPS, and from the department (DCP). The police interview would have supported 3 years of past historical reports and substantiations. Joanne proceeded into a lengthy Family Court trial oblivious of the misfeasance by the officer, but was still awarded sole custody. Six weeks after the orders were delivered; Ella was injured on week-end visitation with the father. Joanne was obligated to report the injury. Officer Thompson was conveniently in charge of the second investigation and concealed, once again, all the abuses, writing that the child made "NIL DISCLOSURES."

Ella should have never been removed from her mother's care in the first place (as the Family Court judge had so ordered for the protection and well-being of the child).

Estimated Costings (over 5 years):

DCP normal operations; staff – case workers, visitation personnel, drivers, admin and general costs, arranging psychological reports, etc. $55,000/annum X 5 years	275,000
DCP costs and staff costs associated to court challenges in Youth Court, Magistrate Court, District Court and Supreme. Court. Case worker and superviser costs of writing and collating 1,000s of pages of court documents, etc. 2018 – $15,000; 2019 and 2020 -- $70,000 (X2); 2021 – $75,000, and 2022 --$30,000	260,000
Payments for reports and court appearances over 5 years to psychologists, reports writers, family consultants and psychiatrists, etc. Allocation: $90,000 (over 5 years)	90,000
SAPOL costs of police officers, meeting, alleged investigations over 2 years, and court appearances. Allocation - $35,000, plus SAPOL'S IIS several alleged investigations and reviews, etc. Allocation: $15,000.	50,000
Time and cost of oversight bodies regarding reviews, alleged investigations, appeals and correspondence, etc. This includes the Ombudsman, APHRA, Commissioner, OPI and ICAC, etc. Allocation: $90,000	90,000
Attorney-general expenditure for legal teams over 5 years. Multiple teams with various hearings across 4 courts, 2 trials, etc. Teams included the Crown barrister, and solicitor (x2); a number of children's lawyers and barristers, and a team for the tort against the social worker. (It is extremely difficult to estimate the costs, but, for example, it was noted that Crown solicitors were allegedly on $30,000/month retainers. Allocation: $750,000 over 5 years (conservative)	750,000
The cost of court days, multiple magistrates and judges across Youth court, magistrate, district and the supreme court over 4-5 years. Allocation over 5 years: $110,000	110,000
Carer costs -- $20,000+ X 5	100,000
Conservative estimate of funds misappropriated:	$1,725,000

Had Officer Thompson reported the allegations in the 2017 interview (and not written "nil disclosures"), these following actions would have unfolded:

(i)   The department and CPS investigators would have been alerted, supporting their 2016 investigations where they had already substantiated abuse.

(ii) The CPS investigator's testimony would have carried weight in Family Court, with the possibly that the trial would have been discontinued.

(iii) Ella would not have been injured in April 2018.

(iv) The spurious allegations by the St Mary's DCP team in 2018 that the mother suffered mental health problems would have been snuffed out, as per the records in their own departmental system.

(v)   Ella would still be with her mother – as ordered by the Family Court judge, and

(vi) The 4 to 5 years of Youth Court; a tort action against a social worker in the Magistrate and District Courts; applications to the Supreme Court, plus an application to the High Court would never have eventuated.

What a catastrophe. Mother and daughter are still apart.

Every dollar expended by the government after May 2018 was a financial deceit on the people of Australia. I have tried to outline conservatively, as best as I can, the financial exploitation over nearly five years. It is astonishing to consider that just one single *unlawful* action set off a train of events that would essentially ruin two lives. The mother, a highly intelligent, feisty, person is destroyed in every conceivable way, and it's difficult to imagine the horror that this courageous child has been subjected to.

Who benefited financially by these actions? Almost everyone!

DCP staff -- from case workers, supervisors, team leaders, and executives – anyone who prepared a continual stream of voluminous, maliciously-damning court documents sprinkled with falsities that facilitated the agenda. Psychologists and other "experts" were assigned to write reports to fall in line with their removals program. The Attorney-general's budget was harvested to pay the salaries of Crown solicitors, barristers, child lawyers and their barristers, magistrates, judges and court costs.

Just one person along this long chain could have said, "Hang on a moment, a crime was committed to initiate all these actions..." But, no one ever did. They were following the script; and the magistrates and judges had every opportunity to provide this child "liberty and security of person..." and "equal protection [under] the law," but they did not.

After her child was removed in 2018, Joanne was under a strict supervised contact order, and she considered it reasonable that the father's contact with his daughter also be supervised (until the matter had been finalized in Youth Court). Concerned for her daughter's safety in 2019, as Ella had told social workers she was fearful of him, Joanne made an application to the Supreme Court for an *ex parte* hearing to request that the father be supervised too – to ensure Ella would not come to any further harm.

Joanne told me the judge entered, holding a piece of paper, and cited an obscure phrase in the Family Court judgment (paragraph 300 plus) that "the mother had exaggerated." It was false anyway as Officer Thompson had lied and had not informed the Family Court of the police interview. (The reality was that Joanne had actually underestimated the extent of the abuses because the officer had kept her in the dark.) The Supreme Court judge ignored the dozen or more egregious abuse reports from the teacher, doctors, psychologist, CPS investigator; and the police interview. He had miraculously "found" the one "exaggerated" phrase that had been parroted by the Crown barrister many times in Youth Court. It would have been almost impossible for him to have found this completely hidden, irrelevant, hearsay-derived phrase in material not submitted. And so the Supreme Court judge quickly dismissed her application.

How could a judge be so reckless with the evidence presented? There were at least 70 pages of compelling mandatory reports discarded for just one hearsay sentence. He was not interested in protecting the young girl, and continued to facilitate unfettered contact (and possible reunification) with the very person Ella said had abused her over several years. Not for a moment did he demonstrate caution.

It became absolutely clear that the judge had been briefed before an ex parte hearing -- either by the department, or by the DCP's legal team. It was an extraordinary and shocking revelation – and proof that even the Supreme Court is no longer independent. One must presume that judges and magistrates are instructed not to tamper with child protection matters – i.e., the child trade.

The government also went to great effort to crush a tort against a social worker for falsifying documents. In the District Court appeal the magistrates gave the case worker 'witness immunity'. Extraordinary! This was a 007 move decision – giving any social worker in Australia immunity from prosecution -- a license to kill (specifically the license to alter documents that could result in a death). We are supposed to have a judiciary that is separated from the other arms of government based on a doctrine known as the separation of powers. We are told that the peace and good order of our society depends heavily upon the maintenance of an independent judiciary, but it's mostly all a lie when comes to children and courts -- and how department staffs are "protected" when they act unlawfully.

These court chronicles demonstrated to me the true power of the hidden hand behind the child protection racket.

"Publicity is the best disinfectant."

-- *Rex Patrick, Transparency Warrior*

Star Chambers

I now know why our fulltime efforts over three-plus years challenging the department in Youth Court, SA, were a fruitless exercise. History has demonstrated that you cannot compete with something that functions like a *Cosa Nostra* operation controlling everything from the playground to the highest levels of government. All of this stems from the fact that the Children's and Youth courts are not operating as courts, but as "Star Chambers" (subservient to the department's agenda). This also made the further challenges in the Magistrate and District Courts, the Supreme Court and the High Court a complete waste of time.

My knowledge of the complexities of the law is rudimentary, but I want to thank (Sir) Graeme Bell for being my mentor over these years – and so in this chapter, I will explain it the best I can. It seems the courts removing children from parents act *functus officio* – i.e, without the powers of jurisdiction to function as they should. These courts operate in complete secrecy allegedly to protect the privacy of a child while really protecting perpetrators and hiding the actions of public servants. The children are the "merchandise," and vulnerable and naïve parents are easy targets. Once they cooperate with the department, they are effortlessly drawn into the court arena as there is the belief that a court is a functioning, fair and independent institution (separate from government). We think judicial officers operate lawfully to hear and resolve disputes, but nothing could be further from the truth. When it comes to Youth Court (South Australia), it is a 'closed' court functioning in a jurisdictional and/or legal void. (For the purposes of this chapter, I will be referring to South Australia, but I imagine it is much the same in other States.)

The closed courts do not seem independent of government and will most definitely assist to suppress or hide child-related crimes by a public officer (as they regularly do in Family Courts). The rules of evidence (Evidence Act) don't apply and matters are resolved "on the balance of probabilities" (e.g., s58—Standard of proof in the *CYPS Act 2017*). That might sound okay, but in reality it's a disaster. Hearsay or the 'bought' opinion from an "expert" trumps all evidence.

And what happened to the presumption of innocence? They don't have to find a parent guilty before sentencing them to a life of social-solitary-dystopia where they are barred from contact with their children -- something equivalent to a life sentence. One mum challenged the magistrate in Youth Court, "If you think I have done something wrong charge me, Your Honour. Please charge me." They wouldn't dare as the misfeasance of public servants would be on display in a regular Magistrate or District (open) court, and it would be impossible to prove that she was an emotional abuser in a normal court.

In Family Court, the judge determines where the child might live, and when and how often the child might see each parent. But in Youth Court SA, the ONLY jurisdiction the magistrate has is 'the removal of the child'. The magistrate is only the SIGNATORY – and has NO jurisdiction for how the child is to be protected or cared for. The department is running the show, and only requires a "rubber stamp." And that removal approval is very easy to obtain. Why would a magistrate defy the Child Protection Department's view (which could be based on the opinion of a 22-year old social worker) if the child is allegedly in need of "protection"?

Of serious concern is that Emotional Abuse was the most commonly reported primary abuse type for substantiations (59%) (aihw.gov.au[51]). There is no legal standing or barometer to gauge emotional abuse; and hearsay or inferences can be used to arraign false accusations against a loving and caring parent. One "off-kilter" accusation (e.g., "the child is not safe in the mother's care") or a lie can damn a good parent and destroy a child's life. Easy as pie – and the deal is done.

Is the magistrate just a RUBBER STAMPER?

The Youth Court magistrate can, however, place "refraining orders" on a mother from going near the school or the carers' home. But once the department (DCP) has guardianship they can do with that child whatever they wish – send the child to live in another State, or change his or her name -- and there is NO WAY to challenge their decision. And it is close to impossible for any minister, commissioner, police official, or corruption oversight bodies, etc., to correct a wrong decision – even the ombudsman. The usual answer is "We are unable to intervene as the matter is before the court" (or the court has dealt with the matter). As the child is under a (continual) court order (or action), does this mean they can NEVER intervene? I guess so.

During Joanne's second trial in Youth Court, her daughter, Ella, made a plea to the magistrate, "I want to go home." But Magistrate Koehn awarded guardianship to the State until she turned 18. (You will read my letter to the Chief Justice in the following chapter.) After trial the DCP St Mary's staff drastically cut contact between Joanne and Ella. (She had called them out as 'child traffickers', and I believe this was their way to punish her and show her "who's boss.") At an appeal hearing, she asked the magistrate to please make the department follow orders (i.e., that mother and daughter should have contact). The magistrate replied, "Sorry, I cannot instruct the department on contact."

This was another light bulb moment for me. The magistrate had accepted the malfeasance of a police officer, and had covered for the department. I think it's clear that the judges and magistrates in the Children's and Youth Courts are SERVANTS to the so-called protection agencies. However, I'm still trying to figure out the legal web. When a child is removed, parents have to appeal the Youth Court decision in the Supreme Court. But if your child is under State guardianship and the department is potentially placing that child in harm's way, it seems impossible to intervene. One mum went to the Supreme Court to challenge the actions of the department, but the Supreme Court judge told her, "I don't have the jurisdiction to alter their decision; you have to go back to Youth Court." But the Youth Court magistrate has no jurisdiction to direct the department -- and the department knows it. So in the Supreme Court, the mum was told there is a void in the law — *lacuna praeter legem*. In Legal Latin, the phrase *praeter legem* "refers to an item that is not regulated by law and therefore is not illegal."

The Children's and Youth Courts seem to be operating in a legal vacuum subservient to the all-powerful cartel-like operations of the service industry. The social workers know they are in control, and that the magistrate is no more than the 'rubber stamper'. I heard a recording of a mother discussing contact with DCP social workers. She hadn't seen her son for many months, and said, "But the magistrate said that the mother [she] should have contact with her son." The social worker replied: "We don't have to listen to the magistrate, as we have the discretion... the department has the discretion if we think you are a risk to your child."

The worst part of this legal void (*praeter legem*) is that (in SA) there is NO RELEASE MECHANISM. I believe the Youth Court magistrate can't 'unstamp' his or her decision. Even when the government is found to have acted unlawfully, one has to move mountains for justice to be done. Although statistics reveal departments do return children, from those I speak to, it is a miracle if a parent wins in court and gets back their child. It seems that the child trade by State government agencies has, in effect... a "NO RETURN POLICY."

Was this complexity and legal void done deliberately? I am now sure — "on the balance of probabilities" — the system and the laws were designed deliberately: to make the laws confusing and convoluted to allow the children's courts to operate in a legal labyrinth, and in SECRET. The State holds a huge advantage, and laws offer far-reaching powers to the Chief Executive (in SA).

It's a Star Chamber with the department essentially facilitating a lucrative child (trafficking) service industry (business), which discourages and constrains ministers and oversight bodies from intervening. I am sure most child removal cases are pre-ordained to fail. (One mum was told by a department supervisor, "Don't bother challenging, the department always wins".) I would go as far as to say that Children's and Youth court is a GAME, where, each day solicitors, barristers, judges and magistrates go through the absurd mockery of court-theatre when the outcome is a *fait accompli*. It's a COMPLETE FARCE. They all play along with the court-sham to pass the days and get paid. Maybe the magistrate in the first hearing could say, "It is most unlikely you will ever win against the department. Over the next two years whilst we all get paid for showing up in this court room, the department will collect evidence against you and see to it that you become emotionally and financially depleted. In two years' time your status as to whether you can care for your child will become questionable, and it will easy for me to award guardianship to the State."

Joanne was told before the trial that she had lost. The trial was a prescribed witch hunt where facts were shredded. She had said years before, "I will never win in Youth Court; they will never allow me to win." Sadly, she was right. They brought in a psychiatrist who made a fool of himself trying to serve their already pre-determined outcome (i.e., guardianship). But it was clear the court was simply a sham and 'gas lighting theatre'.

When deception is at the core of these removals, it is ruthless and malicious -- with absolutely no regard to the well-being of the child or paramountcy principal. Even when criminality by public servants or the deceptions of experts is exposed, the protection agencies and public servants seem unable or unwilling to reverse "the trade" or right a wrong. It's a national disgrace and parliament must challenge the ethics and systems of the child protection operations. In 2022 I wrote, again, to the Hon. Chief Justice Kourakis, South Australia. My letter summarized my observations of the judicial process of a specific case (Joanne's) which I had investigated and assisted for over 4 years.

My Last Letter to the Chief Justice

[Below is a much shortened version of my correspondence to the Chief Justice in July 2022. It's a punishing account of Magistrate Koehn, and I'm sorry he is the focus of this letter. A barrister told me he is a "good man", but once these judicial officers enter Youth Court they seem to operate on a different legal frequency. So in this letter, magistrate Koehn *represents* the collective of magistrates and judges in these children's and youth courts.]

The Hon Chief Justice Kourakis

High Importance

Your Honour,

I have written to you about this case over the last few years, (including 21 April 2021). What happens at 75 Wright Street (Youth Court) is unbelievably wrong. I am writing about the 'same' case – but so many are similar. The mother has Federal sole custody of her child – but Youth Court's Magistrate Koehn has now ordered forced separation until the child is an adult – on malicious speculation. He is robbing the child of the one she loves most in the world, her mum, and the mother of the sacredness of motherhood. The punishment is far worse than prison (for being a protective parent).

I have to point out that the Youth Court is nothing but a STAR CHAMBER, running along the lines of the *Court of Oyer and Terminer* of 1692 – using the equivalent of spectral evidence and pure speculation to "convict" a protective parent to a life of hell. In this instance the magistrate acted so far beyond his powers with such error and irrationality that no reasonable person could EVER arrive at his conclusion. This case is just truly diabolical and is nothing more than 'Abduction of a Child s80' of the *Criminal Law Consolidation Act* as she was removed by deception.

I have remained in the background and mostly silent for nearly four years – waiting for the wheels of justice to be delivered. But it seems that this is not possible in Youth Court. We, a group of concerned Australians (a collective of media persons, advocates and legal researchers), hear of similar cases daily, and we are making these cases known to the public. It is our obligation -- in following the law -- to protect the innocent from state abduction and judicial kidnap. I sincerely hope you will assist us stop the shattering of lives.

I can definitely state this case is only the tip of the ice berg. Where does one begin on how the court ruled? Magistrate Koehn in his judgment made errors in law; based his reasoning on illogicality and 'legal unreasonableness' using defective arguments; acted with bias, and beyond his jurisdiction; violated his statute obligations and the "paramountcy principal". The judgment is "fundamentally defective" and failed to serve process where service of process is required (Lord Greene in *Craig v Kanssen Craig v Kanssen* [1943] 1 KB 256). The order is void as it was a failure of natural justice or injustice to an innocent third party (Lord Denning in *Wiseman v Wiseman* [1953] 1 All ER 601).

It seems, the Youth Court is unable to deliver justice, and is therefore NOT a court. Magistrate Koehn argued in his judgment legal notions that are in DIRECT CONFLICT (e.g., Paragraphs #XY and #YZ cannot exist together.)

> #XY [number not given] The Chief Executive [of the DCP] has established [Really!] that the mother unconsciously influenced the child to falsely believe that she has been sexually and physically abused... This has occurred in the context of the mother suffering a delusion disorder [disproved in court] ... even though the disclosures were not true, I do not find that she [the child] deliberately lied...

> #YZ If all or some of the abuses the child spoke of did occur, the mother has in any case reacted in dysfunctional

ways to it that has caused her distress. In my view that is a form of psychological harm and it certainly exceeds what might be described as a 'response to the ordinary vicissitudes of life'. [Is child sexual abuse considered as an "ordinary" challenge facing a parent?]

The above legal contradiction is not the real concern; the magistrate made so many claims CONTRARY to the facts – thus acting against the child. After a police officer CONCEALED the extreme and alarming abuses in 2017 and 2018, the department removed her daughter on the basis of coaching and mental health. The problem is that her mental health had been cleared many times and she had been cleared of coaching. So as the mother defeated each and every claim; the accusation against her finally morphed into the most IMPOSSIBLE claim of all – something which is not identified in the Act. Her case is along the lines of the Salem Witch trials. (If the woman floated she was executed; and if she drowns she was innocent. Both end in death.)

Expert witness, psychiatrist Dr J B, after clearing the mother twice before in 2016 was brought back (like a 'hired gun') to claim, in a quickly revised diagnosis that the mother has a delusional disorder ("diagnosing from the box" page [redacted] court transcript). There is also zero evidence of this being fact. In cross examination by the mother he stated that his revised diagnosis "would be in error" if there was evidence that [the abuse] may have occurred [which he was deliberately not shown]. When the mother was not in the courtroom he was noted as saying that the mother's calm composure on being constantly accused by him as being delusional was the opposite of what one would expect [that of hostility] from a person with delusion.

That means the claim in #XY is fundamentally defective (i.e., the cause of unconsciously influencing cannot exist); and therefore, logically, the claim is spurious. The Chief Executive had abandoned her original claim that the mother was delusional in believing her child because so many others, too, supported the child. In fact, the DCP held the SAME belief in 2019 as detailed in their submissions:

> "...the child would be at risk of psychological, emotional, physical and sexual harm if returned to the immediate care of the father."

And so the accusation was altered. Thus the sole and final explanation as to why the child spoke of abuses to countless mandatory reporters over three or more years is that her mother has some witch-like quality (that she is unaware of) to unconsciously alter the minds of others permanently – but without knowing it; and that she somehow implanted memories of abuses that she never knew of, nor spoke of, long after the child was removed (the worst of her daughter's disclosures – e.g., private part in mouth -- were only revealed on subpoena in 2019 long after the child was under guardianship). And they claim that her mind-altering abilities must be permanent as her child has consistently refused to retract her allegations and resisted being placed with her father for 4 years (when she was no longer living with her mother). Daughter and mother have been strictly supervised since May 2018... It is an invention; a speculative, far-fetched, unscientific, unmeasurable, and legally unexplainable.

But then the magistrate covers himself with #YZ -- claiming if all or any abuses did occur the mother acted in dysfunctional ways (in front of the child?). Maybe he should describe the appropriate reaction on learning your child's sexual abuse. The magistrate writes that the abuses are "alarming and extreme" (#--) and thus his statement is speculative, and based on malicious innuendo.

The facts reveal the OPPOSITE: that the mother was providing a happy and calm life for the child. For example, after the [date redacted] incident was reported by the grandmother, it is recorded that the mother wanted her daughter to live in calm as reported in the Department's files (Case note XXX) it was reported:

"He [grandfather] advised … All the mother wants is for things to be calm for her [child]…"

There is NO CLAIM against the mother. Of course, the magistrate seems to set aside that: The mother was awarded *sole parental responsibility* by the Family Court (2018). The bona-fide evidence of the child's "3 years of consistent reporting" (2016 to 2018) was to a teacher, police officers, psychologists, doctors, CPS investigators, social workers and family members. It was between father and daughter. Government agencies *substantiated* sexual abuse and exploitation (by the father) after an investigation in 2016 [and this is conveniently ignored by the department in 2018]… Expert/professionals support the child and have documented that she is being authentic. There are 10 affidavits that support the mother as being a "wonderful" and "fantastic" mother.

…Magistrate Koehn accepted and supported those who had concealed of crimes. He accepted tainted evidence from Officer Thompson … The magistrate gave the officer a 'free pass' making excuses for her… *Bellinger v Bellinger* [2003] confirmed that 'the duty of the Court is only to interpret and apply the law not to reform or create it… The magistrate accepted criminal negligence by the department…

My letter continues for several more pages outlining the court's bias; and how the magistrate accepted and utilized testimony from a psychologist who never met the mother or child; and how he disregarded *bona fide* evidence. The Chief Justice never responded, and possibly has not even read my correspondence. However, there seems to be cloud that hangs over these so-called children's courts. It's like a 'frequency', or energy shift that alters those who participate. One mother has described it as a "black magic" spell being cast over the children's courts. It seems so.

PART FOUR

Gas lighting, Insanities and Stranger Things

"Show me a sane man and I will cure him for you."
— *Carl Gustav Jung*

Gas Lighting Menu

The "expert" wields enormous power in the Children's and Youth courts (and Family Court). Their opinions hold more weight than evidence or fact. From my trawling through hundreds of pages of reports from case workers, plus paid professionals – psychologists and psychiatrists, etc., – I have noticed patterns. Disturbing patterns! I'll try breaking them down as best as I can.

(1) Chinese Whispers Reports

I noticed a "progression of opinion" – like Chinese whispers. With each following report the opinion would evolve towards the desired outcome of guardianship by the department. (It is similar the social worker 'relay team' tactic.) Taking the example of a single mother, the first report (#1) might be balanced and the psychologist or consultant might even write positively about the mum and child. The report writer is probably trying to be fair but always straddles both sides of the fence – adding a few words of caution. This fence-sitting is probably done to ensure future work.

The next report (#2) might be an internal review, initiated by a few cautionary sentences in report #1. It will begin the negative damning trail against the mother (or father). It might have facts wrong, or misstatements, but as it is internal, the parent rarely has the opportunity to rebut any falsities.

If the case is being challenged in the children's court, another review (#3) might be called for. A psychiatrist is brought in – and, as an example, does a one hour zoom consult with the mother (yes they have zoom consults). The psych knows how the system works, and would have been given the internal report #2 – which is the department's 'autocue'. Referencing past reports the psych might suggest something like "the mother suffers from paranoid thoughts," or she has "disordered thinking." It's usually not a diagnosis, but a 'leaning' or proposition toward some mental issue. So the "off-the-cuff" pejorative diagnosis is often made in impossibly short interviews (even on zoom), without the required formal psychological testing. It is usually the distress of having the child removed that is the core problem. Being 'worried' about the child, or saying, "I've been up and down since they took him" can twist depression into "the mother displays bipolar tendencies."

In the past, the mum and child might have had a normal and healthy relationship, but by the time the 4th report is submitted to court, it could read, "The mother is unstable... her mental health is a risk to the child... we advocate for her to have no contact with her child." Game over!

(2) The Laundry List

Say, for example, a child has been removed from a mother, often on spurious grounds; the department now has to justify the 'removal' (AFTER the fact) – and so they begin the gas lighting process. You know the saying, "Throw as much shit at the fan, and hope that some sticks" – and that seems to be the tactic. Accusations of hearsay and speculation emerge (and this could be written up by a 22-year-old case worker with minimal experience). Along with some "expert" (e.g., a psychiatrist) the department presents a laundry list of accusations. You defeat one, and they will produce another. I wrote this up in an article, "Emotional Abuse and Trashing a Good Mum,"[52] and these are some of them:

a) Mental Health Disorders: these are the first port of call with accusations ranging from "the mother suffers from an undiagnosed psychiatric disorder"; or she suffers from delusions; psychosis, schizophrenia; or bipolar tendencies (etc.) that "*may* impact the mental health of the child..."

b) Coaching -- If the child made sexual abuse allegations, these are reframed as: "The mother coached the child, making the child believe he/she was abused." If the mother proves this wrong, the claim is altered to "the mother was leading and pressuring the child to speak out." So, was the child abused or not? However, by doing this the direct evidence of the child is downgraded to hearsay evidence by the mother, which is of lower evidentiary value, and is more easily dismissed.

c) Fixations: "...the mother has a fixated view and therefore is a risk of emotionally abusing her child..." (Most often, it is the department that has a fixated view.)

d) Emotional Abuse: the most deceptive and destructive accusation of all is Emotional Abuse. The government's definition is rejecting, terrorizing, or corrupting, etc., but that is NOT what child protection departments define as emotional abuse. A nurturing action can be construed as harmful. Once the child is in OOHC, the social worker might write in a visitation report that, "The child was distressed and tearful on seeing her mother... and this is having a negative impact on the child" which leads to "we advocate reducing access for the mother." The separation is the cause of the child's distress. And they know this.

e) Emotional Incapacity is a clincher. Having traumatized the mother, a social worker can, without substance, write "the mother is now unable to meet the emotional needs of the child at this time..."

f) "Unstable" is a common accusation and is likely caused by the interventions of the department removing the child. If the mum "was tearful..." this is written up as unstable; or if she fights for her child this can be reported as "obstructive." And when "the mother displays anger tendencies" – that is deemed dangerous.

g) Unnatural traits: I've read how love and biological instincts of motherhood can be twisted into a negative, with "the mother—daughter relationship is unnaturally close," or the "mother needs the child to meet her emotional needs," and even demonstrations of enduring love to a newborn can be viewed negatively. This bizarre analysis is all done post-abduction and often by workers that don't have children.

105

h) The discredited Parent Alienation Syndrome (PAS) is a favourite in Family Court advocated by the late Richard Gardner, MD. Dr Rikard-Bell used PAS in his assessments -- potentially removing children from a protective parent after reports of abuse or violence. He discussed his career successes – about 2,000 cases[53] -- on ABC radio.

i) Unworthiness: Other dirty tactics includes the spreading of historical and defamatory rumours -- anything to make out the parent is unworthy or undeserving. This could be cleverly couched as "it is *suspected* the mother was a sex worker in her teens"; or "she/he used drugs as a teen". One mother, an army veteran (third generation military) was suffering PTSD and was caught driving around the block under the influence with her child in the back. She probably lost her license – but she also lost her child.

j) Munchausen Syndrome by Proxy (now known as Factitious Disorder Imposed on Another, FDIA): In one case, a police officer diagnosed the mother as Munchausen's (possibly to avert an investigation). It was an incorrect supposition by someone completely unskilled in medicine, but the department ran with it. A magistrate, thankfully, discarded it as nonsense.

In the above list, I am not referring to drugged out parents; or parents with obviously long-term mental issues. This analysis is after speaking with; and reading material, and watching videos from good parents who would do anything and everything to better the lives of the children they adore. However, there is one more tactic that needs a mention:

(3) Isolation and Estrangement.

This is a brutal tactic when family members or grandparents are manipulated by department staff to turn against, and even blame the protective parent. I have heard this so many times; it becomes devastating especially when family members excuse corruption.

Psychiatric Insanity and the Department

There is the expectation that "Psychiatrists shall uphold the integrity of the medical profession" -- *Code of Ethics*[54] for the Royal Australian and New Zealand College of Psychiatrists (RANZCP). Psychiatrists should never abuse their expertise, and must strive to avoid causing harm to people.

Dr Peter R. Breggin, MD (and Ginger Breggin) coined the phrase, "Psychiatry has a long history of acting as an instrument for psychological, social and political control."[55] Of all the chapters in this book, I think these few on psychiatrists are the most disturbing. And the dereliction of professional ethics, when he or she assumes a duty of care, can forever change a child's or parent's life. I contend many experts were paid "guns-for-hire," and they acted abhorrently. You decide.

I was contacted by a single mum, PJ, in 2019 and then again a few months ago. I have seen videos of her and her 4-year-old son having a happy time in the country, and I've spoken to and met her several times. She has an ethical heart, seems 'switched on', and is a loving mother. She's an ex-court employee, and is familiar with the workings of government. I won't bother to delve into a 30 page history, but it started with her reporting corruption. She thereafter became a 'client' of the department (in 2019) after escaping domestic violence and an episode of alleged substance abuse. However, her baby son was soon returned to her care. Jumping to 2023; after making *another* call to lodge a complaint (whistle-blowing against the government); she was tracked down by the department. She says the police used *extreme* force to remove her son — and it took three officers to prize the desperate child from her. (Her requests to see the police video of the forced removal has been denied.) It's difficult to fathom, but it seems that only AFTER the department had taken her son did they then go about proving — retroactively -- the reason for removing him; forcing her into psychiatric care for several days for an 'assessment'. In a recording, a doctor claims she has "psychotic thinking" as she believes the government is "colluding" to take her son. She replies along the lines, "We'll is my thinking not correct? They've taken my son." Court documents cite a psychiatrist stating that she suffers from chronic paranoid views that the government is corrupt and that they are stealing children. (But government admitted to, and said "sorry" for 'stealing' Aboriginal children.) I and many readers, retired barristers, and child advocates have exactly the same views – and these views are not paranoid thoughts as they are based on FACTS. But, PJ has been denied all contact and has not seen her son since, whilst the department is making an application to keep him until he turns 18.

Surely there could have been a better way to treat mother and child. I'll focus on one recording of a phone call between PJ and the DCP social workers. Desperate to see her son, she reminded the social worker that the magistrate suggested she have contact with him. I covered this part earlier when the social worker replied, "We don't have to listen to the magistrate…" In the phone call, PJ was trying to reason with them, saying there was absolutely no reason for their separation.

SW "What about the drug tests?"

PJ "They've all come back negative, for years."

SW "There was one positive…"

PJ "That was four years ago… but I don't take drugs." [I don't discount that a "send-in" person offered her a joint or other drugs in 2019. I've heard this tactic in other accounts.]

SW "So we will keep testing you over the time of the order…" [What? They've applied for 18 years.]

PJ "Every test I've been made to take over the last few years has been negative."

I am not sure why ALL contact was denied for a seemingly lengthy 'testing period'. With that accusation somewhat countered, the social worker moves down the gas lighting menu.

SW "What about the differential schizophrenia?"

PJ "I haven't got schizophrenia. You can't turn around on a one hour meeting and diagnose someone with schizophrenia." [PJ confirmed that the diagnosis was done after a 20 minute consult with the doctor that said she had "psychotic thinking." She had seen him a total of 40 minutes.]

SW "Differential schizophrenia is not an official diagnosis, but is in line with the symptoms... do you not see the benefits of seeking therapeutic intervention? (pause) How do you expect to treat your mental health and well-being?"

PJ had written to the department several times stating, that her mental health (PTSD) would resolve immediately on the return of her son — and this view was supported by a second opinion. The doctor said that nothing was wrong with her. The discussion moves to the next 'menu item' -- about PJ not taking the 'medication' that she was offered. It was a voluntary order, but a doctor indicated that it might help get her son back.

PJ "Dr B said if I took them, it will help me get my son back."

SW "So you are only following the treatment to get your son back? And not because you think these things need to be addressed?" [As I've written, the core problem is the distress caused by separation -- the actions of the department.]

PJ "Yes."

SW "The concern for the department is that this is not a tick box exercise... You need to meaningfully engage with the therapeutic services... to better your mental health."

PJ: "But, you're the ones ticking off boxes."

SW "You have failed to take your treatment... you were prescribed Olanzapine 10mg."

PJ "I am on a voluntary order so I don't have to take it. She [Dr B] said I don't have to."

SW "It was listed as a treatment recommendation."

PJ "It made me feel suicidal… that's a mental health risk. And I don't have schizophrenia."

PJ's mother interjects, saying they had gone to the hospital for a second opinion.

PJ's Mother "The doctor at the hospital sent her home. She doesn't have schizophrenia. You can't even test it with an MRI — an independent psychiatrist found nothing wrong… she hasn't got schizophrenia"

SW "Correct [about MRI], but it needs a longer period of observation… they've flagged it [schizophrenia] as a possibility…"

This psych is obviously on auto-pilot and under the control of the 'regime'. Can you imagine trying to blackmail a mother (after a 20 minute consult) to take a drug like Olanzapine on a "possibility"? Olanzapine is an antipsychotic medication that's used to treat "health conditions like schizophrenia and bipolar disorder." Side effects include allergic reactions, hyperglycemia, blurry vision, irregular heartbeat, seizures, and thoughts of suicide.

PJ has been placed in a terrible position. If she takes the medication (to "help" get her son back) it confirms for the department records she has mental issue (schizophrenia) — proof enough for them to claim guardianship. I can just imagine the next court hearing, "Your Honour, the mother is on Olanzapine, medication for schizophrenia, and is not yet stable enough for reunification. She has said she has suicidal tendencies." Case over!

And if she doesn't, they withhold her son for non-compliance of a voluntary treatment, for a yet misdiagnosed, vague condition unknown to medical science. At the next court hearing they'd say,

"The mother has refused treatment for her mental disorder, and this would place the child at risk if contact were to resume..." Case over! And if they insist withholding her son for a bogus observation period to check for further negative drug tests, they'd say, "Your Honour, the mother has complied successfully to the drug program, [implying that she was a drug addict] ...but we feel her son is now settled in his placement and it would be too disruptive to move the child back into her care." If she claims the government is corrupt, this will be proof of her paranoia.

God PLEASE help these people! The moment I get a call from a despairing parent, my heart sinks; the trafficking tricks of the departments across the country are endless and brutal. This is what PJ wrote in an email to me (when I mentioned court):

> "That isn't a court that's a brothel. All they will do like they always do, adjourn it. Banking on it each time and dragging it out so all is broken and lost, but they have their money! They have delivered more services. They have their jobs! My job is a mother. My job is to love... And that court [Youth Court, SA] has no heart and no love! It's a ghost ship!

> "I do not use drugs nor will I take their synthetic drugs either and accept that this is heath! It is hell-th! I am not helping them continue with this 'racket' or their insane orders! This is how they get constant consumers and justify their jobs amongst other things. I have watched it long enough! ... This is how they invasively implant themselves and have a stranglehold over you to fuel their need for forced services through tenders, and money laundering pushed through corruptible legislation. What is concerning is that SA Health has almost 300 pages of these tenders... I have been witness to this through the push of legislation, media propaganda in businesses that I worked in and that profit from such happenings for job creation which has led to the deaths of dear colleagues. This is absolutely ridiculous. We know this government is the real plague... Please help me. I need my baby and he needs me! ..."

In another case, this mum approached me regarding the department taking all three of her very young children. She's is an intelligent, articulate and a presentable entrepreneur. Her one son had made disclosures about his father, but in a strange twist, the department turned on the mother and removed her three young children. They then flew the father from interstate and allocated him care of the children, but even in supervised visitation with the mother, the children kept disclosing forms of abuse by the father. This was, of course, carefully and consistently ignored.

I've seen a recording of a zoom meeting between her and the department staff to discuss visitation and the well-being of her children. She was way more articulate and more knowledgeable on aspects of the law than the department supervisor. I kept thinking, "They're not going to like this." A case worker (with a psychology degree) had once said to her, "Do not think by intimidating me with your big words this will get your children back." But that's how this mother speaks (and thinks), and she always had a logical response (challenge) to every action by the department staff. They also warned her about being combative, and made it known they would punish her, for example, for recording meetings and conversation -- which she has the right to do.

Thus, I was not surprised when I was told they forced her to see a psychiatrist, Dr A Y. The staff must have been delighted with the report... it was crushing. This psychiatrist made the most damning mental health assessment through a suggestive ("likely") confusing diagnosis -- diagnosing a "complex multi-personality disorder" over one 90 minute ZOOM call.

When the mum recounted this to me, she said: "According to the DSM (Diagnostic and Statistical Manual of Mental Disorders) this complex condition requires a histological examination with prior records. Dr A Y failed to fulfill the minimum diagnostic requirements according to the manual reference of his own profession." (I quote her verbatim in an ad hoc phone call -- the person who is supposedly cognitively dysfunctional. *Please!!!*)

Begging for a Delusion

This chapter is sourced from my very detailed complaint to AHPRA about a psychiatrist who became a "gun-for-hire" expert witness for the DCP. It is an extraordinary account. I wonder what the department has over these "experts" to let them jeopardize their careers and their profession. But here goes: this is the tale of how Joanne cross-examined her own psychiatrist.

It 2016, after a report by the grandmother, CPS and Families SA investigated whether Joanne's daughter was abused by her father. Families SA removed the father from the home ending their long-term relationship. But as part of the investigation Joanne had to see psychiatrist Dr Jules B. In his report he confirmed that the mother did not suffer from any mental health issues. The government agencies substantiated sexual exploitation by the father; so he went to Family Court to divert any prosecution (a known trick). This resulted in her having to be assessed a second time by Dr J B. He wrote a good report, but did his "fence sitting" tactic in the father's report.

Jump forward; and to re-cap: Officer Thompson had concealed Ella's (the daughter's) allegations; despite this, Joanne was awarded sole custody in Family Court, then her daughter was injured on visitation; the officer then lied about police interview ('nil disclosures'), and so Ella was removed by the DCP. The DCP then tried a "back door custody switch" (which failed); and Joanne challenged the government in a second trial to get Ella back.

Joanne had countered accusations of "coaching"; she had nine supportive affidavits supporting her as a wonderful mother, and an expert witness supporting the child's disclosures in the police interview. There were hundreds of pages of evidence and mandatory reports -- so after four years in various courts there was not a single reason for the government to keep Ella from her care. EXCEPT if they found a yet undiagnosed mental condition – and, you know, the department never wants to lose.

So the DCP and their Crown's legal team decided to bring back the Darth Vader of psychiatry for the Youth Court Star Chamber – with Dr Jules B as their star witness (the same expert witness that had cleared the mother twice before). Dr Jules B took to the stand and, with a DOUBLE-retraction, said he had made mistakes four years ago in his past assessments and presented his new diagnosis (without any meeting or follow-up assessment) that Joanne has a "delusional disorder" with borderline schizophrenia (by thinking her daughter had been abused). *Note: Does this mean all the many professionals that supported the child's claims are also delusional?* For 3 hours he answered the Crown's questions with "the mother has a delusion disorder" based on a document he was shown that morning. Not sure how a physical wound can be a delusion, but maybe he had been BBB'd -- bought, bribed or blackmailed. The department's legal team referenced a 2010 hospital hand-scribbled ADMISSION note (when Joanne was encouraged to attend hospital), which states that she might be having a "psychotic episode … possibly drug induced". (Joanne thinks she might have been discretely given a drug because she was becoming suspicious and vocal about possible sexual abuse.) The Crown deliberately did NOT give Dr J B the 2010 DISCHARGE assessment from the next morning (after tests, and over-night observation), which read, "Some mild features of depression, good support; accepting ACIS support [Acute Community Intervention Service], NIL evidence of psychotic illness… reasonable insight of judgment."

Imagine! The DCP team was dredging up one misleading entry note – a supposition on admission -- from 2010 to keep a child from her mother in 2022. But let me continue with this sorry saga.

The psychiatrist had twice assessed Joanne, as a patient, at one of her most vulnerable times of her life, so 4 years later I don't think he expected a strong, smart and very presentable woman in court with proficient cross examination skills for someone totally untrained. She 'grilled' her former psychiatrist for several hours to 'crack' him. She pointed out to him (and the court) that the DCP had deliberately withheld all evidence of abuse from him. Dr J B finally admitted that "if I was told that the child has been sexually abused then... I would be in error." We know why the DCP never told him that CPS and Families SA had confirmed exploitation and sexual abuse in 2016, nor informed him of the many mandatory reports, or given or shown him the police interview of the child's detailed and compelling allegations. The South Australian Bar Association Conduct Rules, # 82, says "A prosecutor must fairly assist the court to arrive at the truth, must seek impartially to have the whole of the relevant evidence placed intelligibly before the court..." It is deceit of the highest order.

Once Joanne had removed Darth Vader's cloak, the magistrate intervened wanting to move along. He turned to Dr J B and asked him how the mother could be treated and whether and how she could be medicated -- for her (assumed) delusion. (Now remember this is mid trial, before she has put her case forward. Joanne later accused the magistrate of assisting the DCP's view by leading Dr J B's prepared narrative to discuss a medical regime of mind-altering drugs – thus undermining her, and her defense mid-trial.)

The court broke for afternoon tea, and thinking the magistrate might order compulsory treatment, she did not return for the late-afternoon session. When they convened, they seemed puzzled by her departure – "Was she upset?" "No, Your Honour." They continued anyway, giving time for the child's barrister to question Dr J B. They ignored (or maybe just forgot) that they were on transcript. This is what Dr J B said when Joanne was not in the room: He confirmed that he was "diagnosing from the box" and that he had not seen this rare condition much in his career. He then indicated Joanne's calm composure on being constantly accused by him all day as being delusional was the opposite to what one would expect with that condition. He basically admitted that he had tried to invoke a reaction from her, and so demonstrated that she had NO delusional disorder. The magistrate ignored all this as he still accused Joanne of having a delusional disorder (#XY) in his judgment, thus justifying guardianship.

This proved to me that everything was a LIE; that the *Star Chamber* Court is a fraud – and subservient to the child stealing racket.

The Garbage Bag Children

Several years ago I met a wonderful and caring foster couple. I explained their story in an article on Gumshoe News called "Foster Children of The State - The Garbage Bag Children," and this is their story.[56] In another article, "Unimaginable and Hidden Cruelty by Child Protection Departments and Courts," I wrote[57]:

"When you relate these stories to a normal person, their life-experience and their minds cannot fathom the cruelty."

This is about good foster parents and how, with almost no warning, the child department came and expedited an emergency removal of their 7-year-old foster child. They were known to be exemplary carers and the child had considered them as Mummy and Daddy. The pain and distress caused is hard to imagine. I wrote how "The girl was shunted from a privileged and loving home — the only home she knew — to one cluttered with a number of disadvantaged foster kids. She began to self-harm. She was moved again and again, and later denied all contact with her former family."

Jacqueline and Graeme Bowden's story went public, but I heard it first-hand over dinner. The late Professor Freda Briggs AO, Emeritus Professor in Child Development, had advocated their case and was disgusted by the department's (then called Families SA) actions. (A note on Freda: she had begun as a child protection specialist for London's Metropolitan Police (New Scotland Yard); had researched and lectured on child protection and child abuse for 32 years; was an adviser to the Prime Minister, co-inquirer into Archbishop Hollingworth (2003); and child protection consultant to New Zealand Police. She authored or co-authored 20 books.)

She wrote to the department:

"I am also told that her few photographs of life with and before the Bowdens have been removed, that she was banned from taking her photo albums with her, thereby cutting off her past." As Freda learned, foster child K, was brought up as their own child in a privileged Burnside [Adelaide] family and attended a private school (at the Bowdens' expense) with their own younger daughter. The Bowdens also kept the child in contact with her biological family and made tremendous efforts to enable K to reach her potential.

As Freda wrote: "The Bowdens were exemplary carers..."

I continue with Freda's account, in her words:

"On December 13th [2011], two social workers went to the house and told the foster child to pack some of her clothes and take only one of her hundreds of toys because she was going for a 'short drive'. She was given 35 minutes... then taken to another foster home where there were 11 [including foster children, and with K it became 12]...

"The girl K was deprived of her special needs program that was designed for her where she received 4 extra tutors each week; deprived of her private education, her foster sister, her school friends, her activities such as ballet classes, swimming, and gymnastics and even her Christmas presents. The child was lactose intolerant ... On the 14th January 2014, I [Freda] accompanied [the Bowdens] to a meeting called by Families SA senior officer... The officer said that she understood that Graeme and Jacqueline had loved and cared for the child for most of the child's life [nearly 7 years], she loved them and their physical care was exemplary. However, it was made very clear that the Department would never return her..."

[End of Freda]

I call these poor children the Garbage Bag Children. The social workers arrived 2 weeks before Xmas, and told K,

"We're going on a little drive."

The Bowdens were confused, distressed and were frantically

packing and preparing notes on her lactose diet. The social worker said that her clothes and stuff could not be placed in a case or even a shopping bag. It must be placed in a GARBAGE BAG. This becomes a symbol of severing all ties from a past life. But worse, I think, is the dehumanizing effect it has on everyone, especially the child.

That night, when the social workers were taking her away — leading her to the car -- the little seven-year-old said,

"See you, tomorrow mummy."

The social worker cut in,

"…You are never coming back to this house ever again."

The effect on the Bowden's own daughter has been truly profound and damaging. Their lives were ruined. When they challenged the department, their long-standing family business was suddenly surreptitiously affected and later ended. I can only imagine what K must have gone through.

Astonishingly, a year or so after publishing the article on Gumshoe News a comment came up for moderation (as first-time commenters do). I recognized the name in the email, it was K's. I emailed her, and she replied quickly and asked for photos of her 'sister,' and with affection she still called Jacqueline her 'mum'. After a few emails she was fearful of any further communication and that she would be discovered – so she went 'dark'.

I will not detail the story any further, but thankfully, contact with her family was secretly rekindled.

"Where is Benny"

Sipping my latte in my regular coffee shop this morning, I noticed that the front page of *The Australian* (19 September 2023) had a picture of two policemen forcing an Aboriginal teenager into a paddy wagon – with the headline: "This boy is 11, has done nothing wrong but is dragged screaming into a paddy wagon." Here we go again!

There is apparently a video of the incident, where the young lad was trying to be heard. The article, by Christine Middap, said he was standing up for himself and resisting the "removal". "I'm not moving" said Benny. "No thank you... You have no right to touch me." As they dragged him off by his hands and feet, he yelled, "I want to stay here. It's not up to you, it's up to me. I don't want to fucking go."

The child worker who was just observing the forced removal assured Benny, "You haven't done anything wrong." This was not the first time he was taken from foster parents, Tom and Marie. It's been a 13-year journey for them when they agreed to foster Milly and Benny and two older siblings, Jess (not their real names) and another child -- who killed himself whilst living in residential care at the 15.

Two years ago, when Territory Families (in the Northern Territory) was at loggerheads with the foster parents, it did not renew their accreditation. Benny had been placed with them at 7 weeks old, but around the age of 9, the department then extracted Benny from the only home he knew and placed him elsewhere – with zero contact with the only family he knew (like K). Tom and Marie said, "We were not to have any contact with the children, not even explain or say goodbye."

The principal of Benny's school gave a glowing assessment of the foster parents; "Their love and care ...was a constant in his life since he was a baby and with their support we could see that [Benny] had a real shot of a successful life."

The system is unable to care for the well-being of children, and recycled Benny through seven foster placements. In the end, he ran away to be with his sisters and with Tom and Marie — the couple he calls mum and dad.

That's when Territory Families came for him again — with an armed police escort and then made him 'disappear' into the system. Now Benny's birth mother, Maya, is desperately looking for him because she'd said Benny was safe with Tom and Marie.

In the 22 September 2023 update, Middap quotes Rodney Dillon, the Indigenous Advisor for Amnesty International and former member of the Stolen Generation Alliance. He says innocent children locked up in police cages are being treated "worse than stray dogs... If you saw police pick up a stray dog by the legs and throw it in a cage like that, they'd be charged. But they get away with it because it's an Aboriginal person, a defenceless kid."

Correct, but not completely. The child departments across the country (with police support) do this to ALL children.

I was told of one account of how the police (following a family court order) had to chase down and then drag a kid screaming and kicking to the car of her father — the person she had claimed was her abuser. The one female officer who witnessed this later told the mother that it was the most distressing incident of her career.

I mentioned earlier, the recording of a girl who bargained with the Court Sheriff for close to half an hour. The Sheriff said to the mum, "I see hundreds of these cases." The girl, becoming desperate, eventually said she would kill herself if forced into the car with her abuser. Fearing that she might harm herself, they sent her off to a hospital. When asked "Would you kill yourself?" I was told the girl replied, "Of course not, but what do you do if no one will listen to you."

Exposing The Court

Prime Minister, Scott Morrison, in his October 2018 Apology, said, "Too many were told; they just didn't listen. Too many did know; they just didn't act." He was referring to the findings of the *Royal Commission into Institutional Responses to Child Sexual Abuse* that looked into cases, mostly from decades ago. Did he know that, right under his nose, the courts were still not listening to children?

It was in 2018 when I became cognizant of how the courts acted with malice against children. It was difficult to comprehend as I listened to the many accounts of how the Family Court ignored evidence of child sexual abuse and then ordered custody of the children to their abuser. With the support from a few child advocates we came up with 55 questions for a survey which I conducted online from November 5 to December 16, 2018. I was seeking explanations to the anecdotal reports of unfathomable behavior by the authorities regarding the removal of a child from an apparently good protective parent. How could the court order evidence of sexual abuse be destroyed? Note: The survey focused only on family court cases where sexual abuse had been reported. I published a series of articles on the survey's findings[58] on Gumshoe News and they can be sourced via this link:

https://gumshoenews.com/?s=family+court+survey.

The particular answers to questions are enlightening, and often surprising, in showing patterns -- which groups of people tend to believe a child's allegations, or which groups have a history of suppressing evidence. About 70 people responded (mainly protective mothers, some protective fathers and grandparents).

The responders were from all across the country, some in rural regions, and the children, in question, ranged mainly from 2 to 12. I've included some of the more relevant questions (and answers).

One of the most astonishing outcomes was that the Independent child lawyer's (ICLs) hardly ever believed the child's sexual abuse allegations. Imagine that? The person assigned to act for you is consistently acting AGAINST you. Who are these people? The ICL's opinion has sway with the judge or magistrate, but we know many ICLs never met their young clients. This was voiced in the answers to Question 7, 'Believing the child' (covered earlier):

Q7. "Who DID believe your child? Did someone (even one person) from the categories below believe your child?" [71 responders] [MC - multiple choices]. 58 members of the family did, and 41 of the parent's psychologist or psychiatrist believed the child. On the other hand, only 2 ICL's and only 2 judges believe the child.

When the question was reversed to: "Who did NOT believe your child?" -- 49 judges and 47 ICLs did not. Yet only 2 "Your [parent's] psychologist/psychiatrist" did not believe the child. Wow!

Q 9 reveals many -- mostly family -- were, in fact, prevented from speaking or testifying on behalf of the children.

Q10 notes that many police and child protection services did believe the child, but did nothing.

I covered Q15 in an earlier chapter, as to how much money did Family Court cost. The average was from $50,000 to $350,000, with 4 people losing more than $750,000.

Answers to Q16 revealed that 32 lost ownership of a house, 38 lost a job or a business, and 50 found the process put them in debt (74% of responses).

In Q17 -- 97% of responders said crucial evidence of abuse or injury was disregarded; Q18 revealed that, again, it was the ICLs and the judges that set the child sexual abuse aside. Shockingly, 36 responders (55%) said evidence was destroyed (Q19) with the police being the main culprits (Q20).

"Who was the Judge in your case?" (Q25) One respondent said

"I'm scared to divulge… as he is threatening further court action."
Below, are the names that were mentioned in the survey [as written]:

> Carmody, Murphy, Bell, Justice Tree, Judy Turner, Scarlett, Boyle, Magistrate Kaeser, Paul Howard, Johnston, Stewart, Deputy Chief Justice Faulks, Amanda Tonkin, Shane Gill, Justice Rees, Cronin, Judge John Coker, Judge Baker, Judge Kelly, Andrews, Howard, Vasta, Justice Berman, Justice Kirsty McMillan, John G Barlow, Catherine Carew, Johnson, Croker, Loughnan, Forrest, Rees, Cleary, Piter, Coates, Stephen Scarlet, Middleton, Meyers, Magistrate Joe Harman, Stuart, Austin, Justice Tree, Young, Demack, Duncanson, Tree, Harmon, Justice Philip Butchardt, Justice Steven Strickland, Austin, Cronin, Federal Magistrates Jarret and De Mack, Barry, Robert Benjamin, Justice Forrest, Judge Ryan, Berman, Pascoe, Ryan, Coates, Kent, Curtain, Murphy, Justice Kent, Justice Hogan, Judge Cassidy, Justice Forrest, Justice Katherine Carew, Aldridge, Loughnan, Jarrett, and David Monaghan.

I believe the above indicates that this is an embedded culture in Australia. Why did these magistrates and judges seemingly abandon the "best interests" of a child who had reported sexual abuse? Were they following a shadowy instruction to discount the "paramountcy principal" in these cases?

With regard to "experts," (Q26) Dr Rikard Bell's name rose to the surface 15 times.

The go-to accusation of "coaching" (Q28) was in 80% of the cases. Again, the ICLs (with social workers) topped the list for "Who do you believe changed, or falsified reports, or committed perjury?" (Q32).

The ICLs also discouraged reporting the abuse (Q36 and Q38), with police refusing to investigate because the matter was before the Family court? (Q37). This defies logic, as the court relies on the police to investigate -- and there is no lawful reason for the police not to continue to investigate.

There are a few other astonishing revelations. 44% said their "children were asked to reveal their disclosures in an interview with their abuser present?" (Q43); 65% of responders said the "court prevented them from seeking medical or psychological assistance for their child" (Q44), and 50% of ICLs never spoke to the young child clients (Q45).

Q49 listed the sexual abuses, with 29 saying the children had physical injuries. (Well, how do you coach physical injuries?) Q50 revealed this left most the child with behavioural or anger problems. 16 responders said their children tried to run away.

I think the final question (Q55) leans to the integrity of the responders and their answers. When asked: "If you only had ONE choice — what outcome would you vote for?"

- 3% chose financial compensation.
- 43% for a Royal Commission into the Family Court.
- 54% for criminal investigations; prosecutions.

As a side note: Other patterns developed from doing the survey. I learned that some children spoke to their protective parents about being visited and hurt in the middle of the night. One account went like this: "My young boy woke up distressed, saying he was visited by Superman last night, and that Superman hurt him; did things to him." Parents might initially think their children are having a bad dream. But one young lad described to police how his father and friend, disguised in bear masks, raped him. The police did nothing. I began to understand the many tricks used by abusers to disguise their horrendous actions. Parents keep alert!

Time to Face Reality

In 2015, when Senator Bill Heffernan's spoke on the Wood Royal Commission, he said,

> "It's time the Institution of the Law faces reality."[59]

In his 28-pedophile-naming speech he said, "pretty heartbreaking to see what's going on and what's been denied for the last 50 years now being exposed..." and that the institutions have "been compromised." (The speech on YouTube.[60]) He went on:

> "...I have documents here which the Royal Commission has seen to justify that case and in fact every Attorney-general and Attorney-general Ruddock until now has seen some of these documents and they are police documents... We had, sadly, a compromise on the highest of levels. There's a former Prime Minister on this list and it's a police document..."

John Howard placed a 90-year suppression order to prevent the disclosure of the names of 28 high-ranking alleged pedophiles. Bill Heffernan goes on to explain that children are used as tools by the Family Court, and "Family Court judges demonstrate regularly they cannot deal with allegations of child abuse."

He continued:

> "The Wood Royal Commission, as you know Mr Attorney [George Brandis] was about to explore — and it's in the Hansard so it's no great secret — who the legal fraternity people were that used to attend Costellos, the boy brothel club... in Kings Cross. And I've got the list here, and a lot of them are still practising. But the judge of the day, the Commission, decided it was a no-go zone ... 'We'll rise for morning tea' and they never went back to it. ... [the Commissioner] said, 'We've decided not to revisit that issue because the public would lose confidence in our judiciary'..."

A few years ago, a mother of two called me and relayed an account of how half a dozen policemen arrived in combat gear to remove the children from her care – based on a family court order. The judge had not believed the children's disclosures.

The kids apparently pleaded with department social workers to no avail. When the time came to remove the two kids from their home, the eldest bolted and hid overnight at a neighbour's house. The officers left, but returned when the kids were back at home.

Both of them begged not to be taken, describing how they'd be harmed if they left their mum. But they were forcibly removed. The younger child then escaped, and ran for his life, to no avail.

She messaged me this:

> "There is nothing I would not do for my angels. There is no glow in my days anymore. My heart aches like it has been ripped out many times over. Just to hear their voices, or hold onto them. They were crying when I gave them their last kiss. The family court didn't believe them. They are part of the stolen generation."

Nancy Spoke Out

This is an extract of the TRANSCRIPT of US Senator Nancy Schaefer's Speech on CPS Corruption[61] when she spoke at the 2008 Eagle Forum Conference (Eagle Council XXXVII Reports) in Washington, D.C. on 26 September 2008.

"Thank you dear Phyllis, and I thank you to all of you. I have served in the Georgia State Senate for four years ... However, for four years, I've been confronted with families struggling to remove their children from the clutches of Child Protective Services.[62] I wrote a scathing report last year, on the corruption in Child Protective Services, and an update, and copies are out on the table. During the last session of the Georgia General Assembly I introduced Senate Bill 415 relating to juvenile proceedings, and copies of that bill are attached to the report on the tables... for the department of human resources to provide emergency care to a child without a court order to be reduced from seven days to 72 hours. It required a court order to enter the residence of a parent or guardian to seize a child. It called for family court to be open to the public, confidentiality and secrecy and family court protects the wrong people...

"The department of child protective has become a protected empire built on taking children and separating families. This is not to say that there are not those children who do need to be removed from wretched situations and need protection, however, my report is concerned with the children and parents caught up in legal kidnapping. Having worked with probably 300 cases state-wide and hundreds and hundreds across the country and in nearly every state, I'm convinced there is no accountability in Child Protective Services. I've come to several conclusions... one, that poor parents, not always, but often times, are targeted to lose their children because they do not have the wherewithal to hire an attorney and fight the system.

"The case workers and social workers are very often guilty of fraud, they withhold and destroy evidence, they fabricate evidence, and they seek to terminate parental rights unnecessarily. That the separation of families and the snatching of children is growing as the business grows, because state and local governments have grown accustomed to having these taxpayer dollars to balance their ever-growing budgets. That the bureaucracy is huge, look at who is getting paid, state employees, attorneys, courts' investigators, guardian ad litem, court personnel and judges, there are psychologists, therapists, psychiatrists, counselors, foster parents, adoptive parents and on and on.

"All are looking to the children in state custody to provide job security.

"That the adoption and safe families act set in motion first in 1974 by Walter Mondell, and later in 1997 by President Bill Clinton, offered cash bonuses to the states for every child they adopted out of foster care. In order to receive the adoption incentive bonuses, local child protective services would need more children, they must have merchandise, that sells, and they must have plenty so the buyer can choose.

"...Employees work to keep the federal dollars flowing. But that is only the beginning figure in the formula in which each bonus is multiplied by the percentage that the state is managed to exceed its baseline adoption number...

"The tax dollars are being used to keep this gigantic system afloat. Many grandparents have called me to get custody of their grandchildren, before being lost in the system. Grandparents who lose their grandchildren to strangers have lost their own flesh and blood. The children lose their family heritage, and grandparents and parents too, lose the connection of their heirs.

"And the National Centre on Child Abuse and Neglect in 1998 reported that six times more children died in foster care than in the general public. And that once removed to official "safety", these children are more likely to suffer abuse and sexual molestation than the general population. Think what that number is today, ten years later. [That was 15 years ago]

"Here are a couple of recommendations on my list, called for an independent audit of all state child protective services and for a federal congressional hearing on child protective services. Abolish the federal and state financial incentives that have turned child protective services into a business that separates families for money...

"I have witnessed such injustice and harm brought to so many families that I'm not sure if reform of the system is even possible... we must confront the fraud in child protective services. Child protective services seize children using the very system that is paid for by the taxpayer... The bureaucracy of workers benefit financially from a system that converts children into cash while destroying families... No child who emerges from the system can ever be sound or whole. Many disappear, and are never heard from again.

"What is happening in America regarding child protective services is a criminal political phenomenon, and it must be brought to an end..."

Senator Nancy Schaefer

[End of transcript extract]

Nancy was found DEAD at her home in Turnerville, Georgia on March 26, 2010 with a single gunshot wound to her back along with her husband of 52 years, Bruce Schaefer, who was found with a single gunshot wound to his chest.[63]

The Knives Are Out

I wrote an article in December 2019, comparing three South Australian (Adelaide) cases across four decades that had a chilling similarity. A warning: this chapter contains sensitive content, and is about children being cut in the 'ani' with a knife.

This is the account of a woman, a teenage boy and a young girl that walked into a police station and told police officers that they were cut in the bum with a knife and then sexually abused. None of them or their families knew each other, and they went to those police stations separately, and years apart. The only reason these dots are joined, is that they all told me (or their parents did) independently. I have seen and heard their evidence via letters, transcripts, videos and recordings.

None of them was believed by the police or the courts.

The Woman --

My dear and courageous friend, Rachel Vaughan, was 46 when she told me (on camera) how her father, Max McIntyre (deceased), had cut her in the rectum when she was a very young child. I quote from her filmed interview:

"Max came into my room one day… telling me how we going to play this game… [She tried to escape, and] this made him very angry. He grabbed me by the leg and threw me on the bed… He fiddled around in his back pocket. He had a knife, a very oddly shaped knife with a short little handle and curved blade on it… [sharp on the inside]… He held me around the waist very tightly; got the knife and put it into my rectum. I then felt a searing pain on the inside to the left. He then pulled the knife out and undid his belt, his fly and then raped me while I was bleeding…"

In 2009 she went to the police, but it seemed Max, her father, was a protected species. To prove her point, Rachel sought medical confirmation. The nature of Rachel's injury was confirmed by colorectal specialist Professor Nicholas Rieger, MD., yet SAPOL still did nothing.

The Teenage Boy --

When this mum (I'll call her L) reported sexual abuse of her young boys by the father, the police failed to act. L had pleaded with authorities to investigate, but SAPOL, the department and the Ombudsman provided the excuse: "...the matter is before the courts." As a consequence of no investigation, the Family Court went against the mum and awarded the children into the father's care – the person who they alleged abused them. It's a common theme.

The valiant late Professor Freda Briggs had assessed this case, and had exposed the abuse. But for many years, L's children, were forced — against their will — to be separated from the very person that was protecting them, their mum.

I think you might start understanding how the "pass-the-parcel-court-trick" works: "We can't investigate because the matter is before the court"; the court determines there's been no abuse (because no investigation has revealed abuse). And the authorities will never thereafter investigate because the court deemed there was no abuse. Case closed!

The two older brothers (after becoming teenagers) eventually managed (separately) to escape from their perpetrator in mid-2019 and found their way back to their mum. But they were unable to rescue their younger sister. When the police came knocking to take the oldest boy back, he threatened police that he'd kill his father if he was returned. So they let him be.

L told me that they had gone back the police and spoken with a Detective Quinn. With his mother as support, her son asked this officer to arrange a medical to inspect his anal abuse injuries – the same injuries that he had told the police about when he was 5 or 6. Now, in his early teens, he wanted to have a rectal examination to prove the cutting and subsequent rape. I heard the recording where the detective tries to discredit the lad's experience and memory — saying that he needed to have "reasonable suspicion" to investigate. But this young lad courageously refused to be stood over and said that he has abuse injuries on his body, and that he's old enough to demand to be heard.

The Young Girl —

When Ella was 6, 7 and 8-years-old she had told several mandatory reporters that she was abused. In the police interview she detailed how she had been cut in the bum with a knife to Officer Thompson. But, as you now know, the officer concealed the disclosures so there was no police investigation. The officer had however made a 'throw-away' comment about the knife to mum, Joanne. The case was before the Family Court, and so when Joanne was on the stand and relayed what she had been told, the Family Court judge pooh-poohed this 'knife in the bum' as fanciful (and an 'exaggeration' by the mother).

To recap: Ella was injured (cut), Thompson was back on the case and the DCP removed her saying she was never abused. When Joanne asked for a re-investigation, strangely enough, another officer, also with the surname Quinn, reported back to her with his determination "That there was no clear indication that a criminal offense [sexual abuse] had occurred," but admitted that he never listened to the (concealed) police interview.

Consider for a moment:

How could a young boy of 5 or 6 invent such an insane story?

How could a young innocent 7 or 8-year-old girl describe a similar account of what happened to her when she was 5 or 6?

Rachel and these children describe the identical story — a technique obviously known only in pedophile circles. I only learned of this horrific type of abuse when Rachel told me, and since my 2019 article was published, I have learned of a further 4 people who disclosed this happening to them.

I submitted a "Public Interest Disclosure" document to South Australian Ministers Chapman (A-g), Sanderson (Child protection) and Wingard (Police) under the Act that allows for a "person" (member of the public) to make "an appropriate disclosure of environmental and health information…" (5.1), with regard to information "that raises a potential issue of a substantial risk… to the health or safety of the public…" I did this so someone in authority could raise awareness in the police, child services, and the judiciary of this these unusual child abuse injuries. Maybe it could be added to their training, as everyone discounted it as nonsense.

My report, of course, was ignored. No one seemed interested. As I have said: children are at the bottom of the totem pole. I hope, you the reader, is beginning to understand the patterns of thinking and the *modus operandi* of the protection system.

When a young girl discloses egregious abuse she is punished and her life is disastrously disrupted. When a young lad returns back to the foster home where he felt loved and cared for, he is dragged away and put into a paddy wagon like criminal. The legal representatives of children often don't bother meeting them resulting in the court going against their wishes. When the department claims that a whistle-blowing mother has a fixated and disordered view that the government is corrupt, what happens to her child? The child is the one punished by being removed from the only person he knows and loves in the world – and sent off to the Gulag foster care service industry.

In so many of these cases, the actions of departments (and courts) result in the child being psychologically harmed. To consider these actions were done for the child's safety or in 'best interests' is contemptible.

"Law and order exist for the purpose of establishing justice and when they fail in this purpose they become the dangerously structured dams that block the flow of social progress." *--Martin Luther King, Jr.*

History Repeating

In December 2022, I happened to watch the SBS-TV program "Who Do You Think You Are?" The episode was about TV presenter Grant Denyer's ancestor Mary Ann Langley who was imprisoned in 1877 for having burned down some haystacks at the family farm in Adelaide.

An old newspaper story had covered the trial explaining that after Mary's mother died, her father, Charles Langley, used his teenage daughter to alleviate his sexual desires. He had impregnated her resulting in a son (who was six-years-old when it went to trial). Mary admitted to arson but it was out of revenge, "*He has ruined me body and soul*". Grant Denyer broke down after learning about his family's dark history, saying he felt "sick to his stomach." I thank Grant for voicing his disgust, but I wanted to tell him that nothing has changed — especially in South Australia.

impossible. The father's own statement that he had had incestuous relations with her was indirectly confirmed by the statement she made to the police officer, and that supplied the motive for the act of arson. His evidence was that she had to'd him in these words—"I lit the fire." "I wanted," she said, "to burn the old devil out. *I was driven to it; you don't know what we have suffered.*" She added, "I am not sorry for what I have done. *He has ruined me body and soul.*" The Jury, following the direction of Mr. Justice Stow, who tried the case, could not permit the chapter of horrors which had been brought to light — though it must have pleaded hard to their sense of pity for the wretched woman before them—to blind them to the true facts proving the charge against the prisoner, so they found her "guilty." They went,

It went to the Supreme Court and Mary was sentenced to five years in prison for damaging his (their) property. The father got off scot-free, despite having committed incest and rape of a child. In the SBS program, Grant said, "There no justice in it ..." implying that it could never happen now. Mr Denyer, sadly, the situation in the courts is now way worse. Unimaginably worse! How can I say that you may ask?

I and others can provide so many examples of how the police, the so-called child protection departments, and the courts act AGAINST children in the most contemptible ways. The case of Ella is just one example: The Youth Court, SA, was witness to the police interview of the young girl's disclosures; it had heard from an expert with several decades of experience in such cases who fully support Ella's testimony. Yet the DCP still maintained she was never abused – implying she was a liar.

I guarantee to you that this child could NEVER have invented the innocently-told descriptions of what had been done to her. As an award-winning international film director for over four decades, I believe that I'm an EXPERT at identifying a "performance" as opposed to reality. She was relaying her graphic experiences as best she could and her body language displayed her trauma, shame and attempts of disassociation (for over an hour) when she was questioned -- struggling through explanations of the different abuses (e.g., being forced to drink yukky white stuff, having a penis forced in her mouth, bleeding when going to the toilet, etc.).

Officer Thompson kept saying, "Tell me the truth... what happened next... you are in a safe place..." No, she was not in a safe place. She was in a most dangerous place, for we know what happened to her when she told the truth. (The officer even told Joanne after the interview that she'd passed the 'truth test' in the beginning.) But then Thompson CONCEALED the truth and facilitated her abduction from her protective mother – suffering NO consequences for concealing a crime and falsifying her notes.

What makes this case (and so many others) so abhorrent is that when the child 'protection' department and its social workers, the report writers, the department's legal team and the court were presented with all this overwhelming evidence of harm they ignored and discarded it. Let me be clear, they knew this young girl had been abused -- there can be NO other conclusion. These disclosures are a hundred miles *beyond* "reasonable suspicion" or "probability". One or two reports could maybe be seen as a 'probability' – but about 4 years of reporting? (This case would provide every aspect of child non-protection in a training course.)

I will briefly discuss a tort against one social worker (C v M 2021). Joanne sued the case worker in the Magistrate's Court for making false allegations against her mental health and for altering court documents (perjury); i.e., changing a very important line in an updated court submission... from the child is wanting to go home to her mother... to the child does not want to go home, but wants to live with her grandmother. It was an obvious and deliberate alteration (probably under instruction from the supervisor and done to bolster the department's guardianship claim). It was no mistake. And the claim against her mental health was false as the professional assessments demonstrated in the department's own data base. They could never provide proof of their claim.

The tort cycled through the Magistrate Court, but after a numerous court appearances the magistrate threw out the case without hearing the evidence, claiming the case worker must have made the alterations "in negligence" so the mother's case "must fail because of s74(2) of the PSA." Sec 74 of the *Public Sector Act 2009* (2) states "...no civil liability attaches to a person to whom this section applies for an act or omission in the exercise or purported exercise of official powers or functions."

Joanne appealed to the District Court. The appeal judge disagreed with the magistrate's decision, stating in his judgment that "...on the assumption that the respondent acted dishonestly, she is not entitled to the benefit of s 74(2)." But he and the Crown had another trick up their sleeve. And it's a zinger – he granted the case worker "WITNESS IMMUNITY" – i.e., "The immunity granted to a witness or a party from civil suit operates to defeat all of the claims made by the applicant. No civil action can be maintained against a witness for giving false testimony. This immunity extends to evidence prepared, given, adduced or procured in the course of legal proceedings."

Does this mean EVERY single social worker, psychologist and psychiatrist in Australia is immune from perjury or any dishonest act when assisting or reporting in a matter relating to the removal (abduction) of a child? Can you see where I am going with this? This provides a "get out of jail" card for any false report, false testimony, or any false claim against the parent or child -- as every child removal becomes a court matter. Maybe this is proof that this game is a 'child protection racket', as one of the hallmarks for any racket is that the participants are immune from prosecution. *Houston we have a problem!* Well maybe not. I am sure that this nonsense will not last much longer. If she'd reported the truth, then would this have gone to trial? The social worker's malfeasant actions *resulted* in the matter going to trial. In a stunning YouTube video, entitled, "CPS lawyer wants judge to allow social workers to lie"[64] a CPS lawyer wants a US court of three judges to accept that social workers can lie in order to remove a child. The three judges are shocked, one judge saying how could a social worker "possibly believe it appropriate to use perjury and false evidence to impair someone's liberty" (i.e., remove a child). He says it's "mindboggling." *Yes it is!*

But why would they all act against Joanne's daughter as they all did? What could they be hiding? How did they all benefit? Whatever their motivations, they all became complicit in the conspiracy to conceal Officer Thompson's crime and to perjure themselves to abduct a child into State care. The reader must understand that the events described are NOT the exception; they are the rule. The courts enable the lies to continue; plus the ongoing abuse of children while protecting the perpetrators – also making these children available to the wider pedophile community.

Stranger Things and the Sunday Escort

After I published my first article in 2018, my inbox filled up with case histories, and I spoke to many aggrieved and desperate parents on the phone. It was overwhelming; how does one help? This is the minister's job.

I would listen, trying to understand the sheer lunacy of what had unfolded in their lives, but strange patterns began to emerge. A mother would say to me, "I don't want people to think I'm crazy, so I haven't told anyone but I am being followed, watched." There were cases where the department mysteriously asked for drug-test urine samples the night after someone (potentially a 'send-in') offered a substance. I also heard a variety of weird and wonderful accounts of intimidation, harassment, stalking, of hearing voices and mind games. The mind-messing seems to be a tactic to put self-doubt into someone to sabotage their life and mental health.

Many people commented on how people came into their house and moved things. I personally witnessed an object and a mirror being moved in this mum's house whilst we'd gone to court for two hours. It was plainly obvious and hugely unsettling. I had stood before the free-standing mirror moments before leaving, but on returning it had been pulled out eighteen inches from behind a dresser. Break-ins were so common, that this one mum often left the front door unlocked.

I tried to be logical, and part of my brain would keep looking for other realistic possibilities. In the early days of this journey, Joanne had often spoken about being watched; followed. The accounts were prolific, and I would think – "Could this possibly be real?" Surely not! And then, one Sunday, I witnessed it myself, and it became all too real.

I'll call this account "The Sunday Escort".

I was in Adelaide filming Rachel and staying at Joanne's house looking after her dogs over Saturday night. It was a weekend in

March 2019, and she'd lost her daughter 10 months before. Around 9.00 am she called to say she'd just left her boyfriend's, and would be back in 35.

Soon into our conversation Joanne noticed three motorbikes right behind her – right on her tail. The traffic slowed, and one bike roared past and disappeared. We must have chatted for about 15 minutes when she said, "Those two bikes have been tailing me since the [suburb]" Then jokingly, "They've sent an escort." We continued talking, but as she was pulling off the freeway she said, "Nooo, they're following me."

We stayed on the phone and my brain was calculating alternative logical explanations -- but the 'coincidence ratio' declined rapidly as the bikers tracked her through several suburban streets. When Joanne said, "They following me down [her street]," I ran out into the road, got my phone ready and watched the "close escort" approach.

She was deliberately driving slowly (about 35 kph), but even with a completely clear empty road, the bikers were tail gating her. They noticed me snapping one of two pictures (below), and then throttled away at 80 kph. I was stunned, but Joanne wasn't as rattled as me, and said sarcastically, "How good of them to escort me all the way home." Just another day in her life!

I have been running Gumshoe News since 2013 and was aware of 'targeted individuals.' Though I remained somewhat skeptical, so many parents described similar patterns of disruption.

I'll cite another crazy incident. A few years before, Joanne had a little bingle which was dealt with by insurance. A few days before the expiry period of the three years period, the elderly driver sued her for negligent driving (reckless endangerment, I think it was) for rear-ending. She called me and said, "I think they are trying to give me a criminal record so they have an excuse to keep [my daughter]." I reviewed the claim.

After nearly three years the late-70s gent had decided to sue for back ache and loss of libido -- and the suffering this caused him and his wife's sex life. (Strangely his unusual surname was that of one of the social workers.) I offered to write a response as loss of libido could be caused from many things like alcohol, smoking, poor health and age. I searched his name (three Christian names and a surname) and what did I find? Ancestry claimed he was deceased. I wrote the short response for Joanne to submit to the court with point 1 being, "Could the Applicant provide proof of life" followed by several other points.

It was not long before a lawyer called, saying "Not to worry" she would handle everything. Joanne declined her assistance saying that the "Applicant is wanting a charge of criminal negligence against me for a small bingle." The lawyer ignored this and started taking over the case even though she was made aware that the Applicant was deceased. Joanne had to inform the court that this random lawyer was not representing her. They had one final heated conversation where Joanne cautioned her once again that a "dead man" had made the application to the court against her. The woman seemed unfussed. However, a few weeks later a letter arrived; the matter was quietly withdrawn.

I always wondered whether this was to target and damage her, or was it coincidence – and just an insurance scam.

As I traversed this five year journey, I had the realization that I was living through a two-pronged WAR — both a physical and spiritual war on parents and children. And all the tactics of war are deployed in the 'protection racket' — from 'ambushing', 'scorched earth', 'shock and awe', 'divide and conquer' and 'attrition warfare'. It seems the departments want to win at all costs. And as the saying goes...

"All warfare is based on deception." --*Sun Tzu*

The Fire Alarm & Three Sumo Wrestlers

I have mulled over this chapter for some time as to whether to include it in the book. It's a long complex story, but in line with the *Stranger Things* series that happened along this journey, so I've condensed it into an appetizer.

It was January 2019, and Joanna was to attend a meeting with the DCP to discuss her mental health. They had removed her daughter eight months previously (in violation of the family court order). And to recap: Joanne had passed all previous mental health assessments; and the police officer, having concealed the child's abuse allegations, claimed in her notes, that the mother (whom she did not know) had a mental problem. It was a deceptive and invented lie and a fraud upon the court.

We thought it might be a good idea if I attended the meeting as the support person – and this is this meeting I discussed in the *Schadenfreude* chapter. I'm missing another chunk of weirdness, but to stay on track, another supporter/advocate drove us to the DCP St Mary's offices. As we parked, Joanne passed me a water bottle from the back seat in an opened but resealed bottle (the supporter had brought them in an Esky). I reached back from the front passenger seat and the woman said, "No, no… that's not Dee's, give her the flower one".

I took my water (Joanne left her plain bottle) and the two of us announced ourselves and sat in the stark, empty waiting room. It was mid-afternoon and Joanne commented how smartly dressed the social workers were. Then three large women (I called them the three sumo wrestlers), one carrying a sizable bag (satchel), arrived and announced themselves. Just loud enough for us to hear, one of the women said, "We're from AFIS (or ACIS) and here to see Catherine Taylor". I later tried to find out if a woman of that name worked there, but could not. Were they to see Chief Executive Cathy Taylor (who would normally be isolated in her high-rise tower in the city)?

Anyway, we were ushered into the meeting room with Ms Moses and Talbot (as previously described in the *Schadenfreude* chapter). It began with, "We're holding this meeting as we have concerns for your mental health" (or similar). Joanne replied, "But I have passed all mental health assessments."

Then the focus turned to me; who was I? I said that I was a filmmaker, had made *The Jammed* on sex trafficking, and was just supporting Joanne. Ms Talbot pushed her chair back. I'm not exactly sure how long it took – but not long. The FIRE ALARM went off – and not the usual "this is a drill" announcement. No one moved for some time. I wondered why they didn't move, and I eventually said, "Should we take the meeting outside?" Talbot got up and left – returning a minute later, saying it's been sorted (a false alarm).

When she sat down, I had the overwhelming feeling that the meeting was over, but we continued anyway. I asked, "Can you produce any professional's report backing your mental health claim?" "We have privileged information" which they were not going to share. It was of course a spurious claim as they never had anything, only the accusations of her ex-partner who wanted to cover up the abuse. I tried to explain what I had learned, and the connection between Rachel's story and Joanne's daughter. Both had identified the same white bearded perpetrator, and this was in a police report. It was a fruitless exercise, as this was obviously side-tracking the agenda.

After the meeting wrapped up, Joanne and I looked at each other, and we both had the sense that my presence had foiled some plan. I'm sure the meeting was monitored and recorded. Had they held a meeting to specifically provoke Joanne about her mental health? They knew she would fire up and challenge them, as she had done in meetings before. So were the three sumo wrestlers from mental health (Acute Community Intervention Service, ACIS) so that they could administer a sedative if needed, and escort her to a psych hospital for observation? And was the Chief present to surveil this event? I would never find out, but last year a whistleblower confirmed that this is what they do, and that there's a button under the table to initiate an alarm. Also, by early 2019, I had heard of a number of cases where either the department or the court would order a mother into a psych hospital for "observation". Many were given drugs for some random alleged disorder. Maybe it was simply to make them appear dependent on some medication. Of course, just the stigma of being admitted and detained for psychiatric care usually destroyed a mother's chances of getting her children back.

(This had been tried on Joanna four years previously (2015). When her daughter spoke of sexual abuse, Joanne had called CARL and her ex called ACIS. A mental health nurse arrived and intercepted her call with the CARL operator. They forced her to the local hospital for observation, but the hospital psych quickly cleared her and sent her home.)

After the January 2019 meeting we met up with the support person and together picked up takeaway for sunset on the beach. Joanne had taken about two bites when she suddenly felt violently ill, and had to race to the toilet to throw up. It was so sudden that I kept wondering; had someone poisoned her food? Impossible!

That night she was still quite sick, and I asked what might have happened. She recalled she had taken a swig from the pre-opened water bottle before climbing out of the car with the food. My mind was spinning. She also mentioned that she is allergic to opioids. I kept thinking – was her water bottle spiked? Had she been taken to a psych hospital with opioids in her system, in combination along with a mental health accusation, it would have been a slam dunk case against her. Case over!

Joanne felt she had dodged another bullet, but I would never quite know what was planned for her that day.

The Fabricated Employee Pass

The DCP (Department for Child Protection) are sending their social workers out with fraudulent Employee Passes.

In June 2019, and my trip to Adelaide overlapped with Joanne's one-hour supervised access (visitation) at her home. I'm told the female case worker arrived with her child, then after about 10 minutes a second 'social worker', a young man, arrived to supervise. The case worker left and returned at the end of the hour.

I was at Joanne's the next day when she was cleaning the lounge and discovered the male social worker's ID pass in the cushions of the couch. On inspecting it, she noticed several aberrations. The ID easily peeled off to reveal another ID below. Both visible and concealed passes had the same pass/card number, with the top pass having expired.

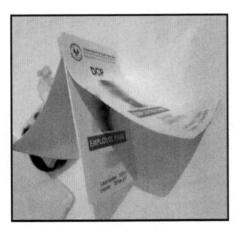

Joanne phoned the department and spoke to someone about the protocols for the Employment Passes, asking: would an ID card be assigned to more than one social worker? Do they recycle cards, or share numbers? Are ID stickers placed over existing cards? It would seem strange that a department with a $500 million-plus budget would recycle ID cards. The woman confirmed that they do not reuse social workers cards; and they do not reuse card numbers as each social worker is assigned a specific number with an expiry date.

Joanne had found a fraudulent pass.

She called St Mary's DCP and asked to speak to Duncan (the person identified in the top pass). Funnily, Duncan had absolutely NO recall of the supervised visitation several days before, and was unaware that his pass was even lost. And he had no answers when asked why he had an expired pass or was sharing an ID number. After about 2 minutes into the conversation he then faked it by saying, "Yeah, yeah… okay, now I get you… Okay now I know who you are." BS!

It didn't take long before 'Duncan' and the female supervisor, Ms Talbot, were at Joanne's house -- very keen to retrieve the fake pass. Joanne made an excuse not to hand it over. It was night, and her porch light was not working, and 'Duncan' hung in the shadows. Joanne called me later, "I don't think it was him, this guy seemed shorter." It was clear DCP staffs were using fake passes for random people to supervise children. Joanne tried to report and expose the use of fraudulent passes, but no one was interested. Instead, SAPOL called her and asked for the pass back.

It was not that long ago that the department (when it was called Families SA) suffered similar failings in the system. In August 2016, Shannon McCoole, a carer, was administrating a sophisticated global child pornography website. At that time, SA's Opposition Leader Steven Marshall (who later became premier) criticized Premier Jay Weatherill's role in the protection of state children, and said "He ran the system. He defended the system and now he must take ultimate responsibility and resign." I complained to Premier Steve Marshall several times about his government's failings, but of course he did nothing. Maybe he should have resigned.

"Feeling love and peace when my mum is nearby giving me hugs and kisses" --*A child's note*

For a decade of her childhood, 2018 - 2028, she will never get the love and peace of a goodnight hug and kiss from her mum.

The Drunken Sailor

Though I have many tales, I will add one more to the *Stranger Things* series. I am hesitant, but I feel this account needs to be aired in case others have had similar experiences.

Over two or more years, I spoke to Joanne most days. I knew the most traumatic time for her when she visited her daughter under strict supervision for one hour at the St Mary's office in Adelaide (this was either every week, or every fortnight depending on how much they decided to punish her). I have been told the "access" room has a big one-way window through which social workers, supervisors or psychologists can observe parent and child – like lab rats. To a good and loving parent, this is a most humiliating experience.

I made a point of phoning her just before access, and she'd call when she left the building. The distress of having to be supervised, controlled, and monitored causes and exacerbates the heart ache of forced separation. The grief is, I'm sure, equivalent to a death of a family member. Joanne often said their loving mother—daughter relationship had turned into a brutal weekly or bi-monthly side-show – with social workers attempting to discredit every move in a completely artificial and detrimental environment.

It was around June 2020 that Joanne emerged saying that she had got dizzy and felt odd during her visitation. It was a visit or two later that she came out saying she thought she had blacked out. At no other time would she describe such sensations. I thought; maybe stress -- but why now after three years of weekly or fortnightly visitations? With years of researching, writing and editing Gumshoe News, those who know me would guess my mind was ticking over.

I gave it no more thought, and it was in August [date redacted] that I gave her a quick call before her visitation. She'd been busy and it was a brief call, with "Call you after."

An hour passed; then my phone rang.

Joanne was calling as she was exiting the DCP St Mary's building. She was highly distressed. Her speech was slurred and she was saying something about blanking out. I immediately knew something was wrong and found and old phone and started recording about a minute into our conversation.

She was disorientated and upset, saying, "I've not felt ill all day." Joanne described how she and her daughter were on the couch together and then moved to the table to play a game (sitting opposite each other) -- and that's when she suddenly started to feel very strange. She described how she blanked out about three times halfway through the visitation session, with her daughter asking, "You okay mum?" Joanne described how she was swaying and staggering out of the DCP building like a drunken sailor; "This is so f**ked, I feel like I've drunk 2 bottles of wine" and "They're going to write up the shittiest report ever..."

I had suspicions in the back of my mind, and asked her to describe any symptoms. She said her throat had suddenly become sore in the session, and was still sore; "I hate this so much, and now I have a sore throat too"... "I've been fine all day." She had a stabbing pain in her left shoulder blade and her temple; and the top of her spine was hurting; "I've never experienced anything like that ... it was the worst thing in the world," and "I feel yuk now." She described how her eyes felt weird and blurry; she felt dizzy and for a short time "discombobulated".

Within a few minutes of speaking to me her speech improved. She had quickly stopped slurring, and said her vision had improved. Within about 8 minutes she'd started to feel better and began to sound like her normal self. Before we ended the call (which lasted about 15 minutes), she casually said again how they were going to write a "terrible report".

I had never come across this before, and in trying to think of all possible explanations; only one seemed to be logical. I discounted trauma and stress as she'd been through this routine for 3 years. I contacted Barry Trower in the UK -- a retired British physicist who was a microwave weapons expert (for MI6) and possibly one of the most knowledgeable persons on this globe with regard to Electromagnetic Frequency Weapons. He thought the symptoms were in line, but just couldn't wrap his head around the idea that a child department might be deploying these tactics.

I also contacted Ray Broomhall, a barrister in Tasmania specializing in legal cases with regard to 5G and harm caused by radio-frequency and electromagnetic fields. He was most helpful and described how they used cheap sound weapons (like the 'Mosquito') in Queensland -- used to transmit unheard frequencies that cause distress symptoms to move people (e.g., the homeless) away from certain city shopping areas at night. But tweak the frequency and you can black someone out, and these sound weapons can be bought off the internet for a few hundred dollars.

I have no idea what happened at the DCP that day. I was reluctant to add this chapter – except that maybe it might have happened to others, and they can come forward.

But on cue, Joanne was right again. She had a pre-trial court hearing a few weeks later – and as she predicted, the DCP submitted a short submission that described that visitation. They submitted, "The mother arrived for access drunk or possibly on drugs." They were, once again, trying anything to further discredit her and demonstrate her unworthiness as a mother to the magistrate to disrupt her chances for reunification.

I immediate wrote up a true statement, and got it signed at the local police station. I reviewed my phone log and stated that on the Tuesday of visitation I spoke to the mother at 9:53, 10:44, 11.05, and 14:55hrs. (We were working on a document.) When I called just before visitation at 15:57hrs (3:27pm SA time), she was completely fine. However, in the call on the hour (17:02hrs) she was slurring and she said she felt ill. I avoided any conspiratorial suggestions and wrote that she quickly recovered and was back to normal in 10 minutes.

In the statement I made a point of saying that I had recorded our conversation.

At the start of the hearing, the Crown (for the DCP) apparently voiced his concerns about the mother, and quickly pointed to the submitted statement by the DCP social worker of the "drunken" mother at visitation – *just* as Joanne had predicted. She stood up and addressed His Honour, requesting to enter a signed statement from a friend. My statement was apparently handed to the Crown, the ICL and court stating that I had RECORDED our phone call after she excited the building slurring and feeling ill but that within about 10 minutes she was completely back to normal.

Can you believe it, that August visitation or drunkenness was *never* mentioned again? They had gone through the entire gas lighting menu over the years, from mental health disorders, coaching, leading and pressuring, fixations, emotional abuse, psychological abuse, "the mother—daughter relationship is unnaturally close," "she needs her child to meet her emotional needs"... but none of these claims ever stuck. She had proof that she never coached; she had several positive mental health assessments -- so did they finally resort to proving her a druggie or drunkard?

But that failed, so it seems they spun the Wheel of Misfortune and decided to buy-in the opinion of Dr J B (described in the chapter '*Begging for a Delusion*').

It sends chills down me when I consider that *maybe* my proposition of them using some disabling weapon might be correct. It's plain to see that they use psychiatrists to claim a parent is 'disabled'. So could 'they' be disabling or "discombobulating" protective parents to discredit them – all for a trade? I sincerely hope not.

PART FIVE

Prosecuting the 'protectors' of children.

"As children, my siblings and I experienced torture... The cover-up was perpetrated by nuns and the state social worker. Their betrayal broke my spirit and robbed me of joy... What if only one adult had fought for me? I can't help but ponder how different my life may have been had someone like Dr Pridgeon intervened..."

--Belinda Paris (aka Binni) from Everybody Knows

Operation No-ethics

The *Royal Commission into Institutional Responses to Child Sexual Abuse* believed the 8,000 victims of historical abuse cases -- so why do the courts not believe the children now? In his apology, Prime Minister Scott Morrison said,

> "And again today we say sorry—to the children we failed, sorry; to the parents whose trust was betrayed and who have struggled to pick up the pieces, sorry; to the whistleblowers who we did not listen to, sorry..." And, "...we can *promise* a country where we commit to hear and believe our children, to work together to keep children safe, to trust them and, most of all, to respect their innocence."

The promise to "hear and believe our children" was broken before it was spoken. I wrote to the PM's office many times and they were impotent to help. This leads me to the sorry saga of Operation Noetic and the so-called "child stealers."

A group of people were listening and trying to keep children safe. A doctor, Dr William Russell Pridgeon, and his friend, Patrick O'Dea (both in their 60s and originally from 'Rhodesia'), plus other mothers and grandparents were trying to support and prevent children abandoned by police and the courts from further sexual abuse and suffering. I first learned about Russell and Patrick in 2018 when the AFP arrested them. The presstitute media were there, on hand, to photograph and publicise the arrests -- and this is what was they published in mainstream media:

> "Doctor accused of masterminding child-stealing syndicate granted bail in Brisbane" ... and financier "of a network that smuggled women and children around Australia..." "Members of alleged child-stealing syndicate committed to stand trial... accused of helping women abduct children..." --ABC

It was essentially a narrative to protect pedophiles, their protectors and enablers: those people who had concealed child sexual abuse.

This all began many years ago, when two young girls disclosed sexual abuse to a number of people. It appears that members of the Police and the ICL hid the reports and/or prevented them from being available to the Family Court. The mother (who Russell names as "Charlie") was unable to protect her daughters after the Family Court awarded custody to the father – the person who the children claimed had abused them. Out of desperation Charlie went to the school and her children left with her willingly, and going "on the run" was violating a Family Court order.

Russell, who had a GP practice in Grafton, treated the girls for agonizingly painful genital ulcers and rectal bleeding. The two girls appeared to be undernourished, pale and small for their age; but they would not allow him to examine them. In Russell's experience, the recurrent genital ulcers were almost certainly genital herpes, so he provided appropriate treatment, including anti-viral medication.

As Russell describes in Chapter 8 of his stunning book, "Everybody Knows":

> "Charlie" was arrested on 4 April 2018; she had apparently been under surveillance by Australian Federal Police for some time... for 2 years (as they told the press), so they must have known everything we did about the children's abuse. Nonetheless, they drove the children straight back to the abusive father, the man whom the children had clearly and repeatedly identified as their abuser... When questioned later about their failure to investigate the children's abuse and their failure to protect these children, AFP Sgt Louise McGregor answered: "It is not in our remit."

Russell writes, "They simply don't see child rape as an issue." He became frantic with worry about the twins, and eventually wrote to the Queensland Minister for Child Safety, Hon Di Farmer (cc'd to the QLD Minister of Police, the Federal Attorney General, the shadow ministers, and several other eminent people). He identified himself as a person who had sheltered Charlie and her children; describing the children's abuse and how the authorities had betrayed them.

This is an extract from Russell's LETTER:

Hon Dianne Farmer, Minister of Child Safety, QLD.

"Dear Ms Farmer,

My name is Dr William Russell Massingham Pridgeon... I have been a medical practitioner for 38 years. I am a Fellow of the Royal Australian College of General Practitioners.

I write to you on the most desperately urgent matter. I am deeply concerned about the immediate safety and well-being of the [Redacted] twins, now 11 years old, who have been fugitives from Australian law after their mother...

I am one of many people who sheltered and protected them, in the four years that they were free of ongoing abuse... This was one of the greatest privileges of my life to be able to help these children escape the horrific abuse inflicted upon them by fiends, and enabled by rogue Judges, lawyers and Policemen who actively hid the truth, ignored evidence, and facilitated child rape, effectively trafficking these children to pedophiles... [He describes the injuries and rectal bleeding]

The father has a history of violence and abuse towards the mother and the girls. Unbelievably, Federal Magistrate John Coker, awarded sole custody to the father while there were AVO's in place against him [for his daughters]. At no time were the people who had heard the children's disclosures of sexual abuse allowed to testify. These children disclosed their physical and sexual abuse on numerous occasions: there were more than 40 disclosures to 14 different adults, including child psychologists, occupational therapists, general practitioners, other professionals, family and friends. These mandatory reports were ignored... When the supervisors reported the children's disclosures to the ICL, she passed the information to the father immediately. The children reported being punished for each disclosure, yet they continued to disclose. Eventually the supervisors stopped reporting the disclosures because they feared for the children.

It is difficult to imagine a situation where there has been so much malfeasance by those public servants who are entrusted to protect children, yet as I have found out as I have become more and more involved in child protection, these scenarios are commonplace and thousands upon thousands of children have been trafficked by rogue judges in the Family Court, with the cooperation of very sinister Independent Children's Lawyers and corrupt Court Reporters...

Minister, it is within your power to rescue these children with the stroke of a pen. You are directly responsible for the safety and wellbeing of these children. Please do your duty immediately... There is an army of protective parents who have watched their children trafficked for abuse. This crime will not be hidden any more. I am absolutely begging you to act immediately, without warning, and retrieve these children to a place of safety, where they can once more be safe.

Yours sincerely

Dr Russell Pridgeon"

[End of letter]

The only response Russell received from the Minister Farmer was to be notified that his emails were blocked. By now you probably understand how the courts facilitate this 'racket'.

Russell sent 4 more letters to Ms Farmer, using other email addresses, but each time the new emails were blocked. His last letter (number 5) had a warning for the minister:

"Dear Ms Farmer,

This is my fifth communication with you... I have pointed out to you that your failure to protect these children when there is an enormous amount of prima face evidence of previous harm, and of immediate risk of harm, puts you in breach of your ministerial duties and obligations, and this makes you guilty of malfeasance. You risk losing the legal protections afforded you by your ministerial office and becoming personally liable...

You are surely aware of the legal actions being taken against George Pell and other senior catholic clerics who also failed in their duty to take timely and effective action to prevent ongoing harm to children... Do you think Minister that you are somehow in a different situation to these priests?

I have never seen such a blatant cover up in my years... Now there is a wall of silence from your ministry and from everyone else. I can only imagine that you are under intense pressure from very powerful people."

[End of letter extract]

As I wrote earlier, I think the ministers have nothing to do with child protection and are kept at arm's length from tampering with the business of the child trading. Any child minister can prove me wrong and demonstrate how they oversee child protection -- but doing so would expose them to criminal negligence. It could be shown that they refused to act when alerted to the criminality of staff and evidence of sexual abuses.

The Doctrine of *Jus Necessitatis*:

The term "necessity" is defined in Black's law dictionary as a controlling force; irresistible compulsion; a power or impulse so great that it admits no choice of conduct. This doctrine is based on '*Salus populi suprema lex esto*' which means that the welfare of people must be supreme. The doctrine of the *jus necessitatis* recognizes that the law has to be broken to achieve a greater good.

Prosecuting Protectors

I attended a court hearing in Brisbane in 2019 when Russell was charged with child stealing. He exited the court and addressed the media. None of it, of course, made it to the general public. This is an extract of the speech I filmed[65]:

"This case is not about child stealing, it is about child protection. It's about the desperate efforts of good people; good law-abiding Australians, desperately trying to protect children from the worst sort of sexual abuse... There is no law in Australia against protecting children from rape... If we didn't protect these children we would be breaking the law. The criminal code [s286], demands that we protect children, keep them safe, and we've done that, yet we are being charged with crimes. The people who have abused these children are not being charged, they are being protected...

"...The AFP knows the full effect of these children's abuse. They have access to the police databases. They have taken our computers, and have taken all our documentation... and evidence of the children's abuse. Yet they do nothing, yet they continue to lie about the children's abuse... Our Prime Minister, Scott Morrison, promised the children of Australia, that they would be believed, and they would be protected, and that's what we did... We believed them and we protected them. This is a very dark moment in the history of the Australian Federal Police. Their behaviour is appalling. They have shamed Australia." [End of speech]

None of this made mainstream news. I was told that some of the media cameras filming Russell were not even switched on.

There is a second unconnected case that was drawn into this so-called 'conspiracy'. Despite a grandmother ("GA") having lawful custody of her grandson at the time (awarded by the Family Court), she was also prosecuted. She had withheld him from the father for some days after the young lad had disclosed abuses. She was arrested and detained (despite there never having being a recovery order) and the police prevented her from appearing in family court. The grandmother's knowledge of the child's abuse was concealed from the court, and the barrister acting for the ICL (children's lawyer) advised that court that there were no allegations of child sexual abuse. As a result her grandson was sent back to live with the person whom he had identified as his abuser. It was only discovered later -- like Joanne's case -- that a police officer had concealed and lied about the disclosures of abuse.

In Professor Freda Briggs' report (advocating for 'Charlie's' two girls), she wrote:

> "For a period of eighteen months, the girls have been disclosing child sexual abuse to at least thirteen different people... Alarmingly, the transcript shows... the mother was instructed to dismiss future disclosures of sexual abuse; told that future allegations of sexual abuse will not be investigated; if the mother examines their genitals when they complain of soreness, she will be arrested for an undisclosed crime; police officers and safety officer repeatedly gave the mother a guarantee that the children have never been abused... [and] that the father is safe and the children are safe with him. I have read 93 reports written by thirteen contact supervisors."

One has to wonder why Russell and Patrick were targeted when other supporters were not. Was it because they had started the Australian Anti-paedophile Party to expose the corruption and child trafficking within the family court? With regard to Russell, the CDPP had to withdraw 5 out of the 7 charges (thanks to Graeme Bell) as they simply could not be sustained. The charges remaining are a "conspiracy to defeat the course of justice." *Really!* Who is really involved in the conspiracy – the conspiracy to defeat the course by suppressing evidence of child abuse?

"Everybody Knows"

"Everybody Knows" is the ground breaking book by Russell, (Dr William Russell Pridgeon) where he exposes the denial of and inaction about child sexual abuse in Australia. It's been a NUMBER ONE best seller on Amazon for some time. When the court found out that it had been published (overseas), it was like throwing a grenade into a gaggle of turkeys.

I mean, you can't have the truth coming out, can you?

Russell writes, "...Sexual abuse of children, most particularly incestuous sexual abuse, has been effectively decriminalized. Granted, the laws against sexual abuse of children remain on the statute books, and may even have been strengthened, but they are simply not being applied." The outcome of this is that the perpetrator gets protection.

Russell had emigrated from Rhodesia (Zimbabwe) to New Zealand and then to the land Down Under, starting a general practice in Grafton. His first knowledge of pedophilia in Australia came in 2004, but by 2013, he was in touch with Professor Freda Briggs, the nation's leading expert on child abuse. This is when she asked him to help the mother and her twin daughters that ultimately led to Russell being charged. He describes why he founded a Political Party (Anti-pedophile Party with Patrick O'Dea), got arrested, and lost his medical license (now reversed). He so clearly explains how the legal system fails children, where hearsay overrides expert reports and evidence. When the court prevents the truth from being presented, you know there's a problem.

What has happened to Russell, Patrick and the others is a terrifying journey of injustice. It means: even if you have proof that public servants put children in harm's way you cannot protect them. Their case (*The King v Patrick Finbar McGarry O'Dea, William Russell Massingham Pridgeon*) is ongoing and the government seems intent on jailing the protectors of children.

I attended two of the Operation Noetic court hearings in Brisbane earlier this year, 2023, and witnessed the theatre of the court. Russell, Patrick and grandmother GA were morally compelled to protect these children from child abuse. s286 *QLD Criminal Code 1899* provides a perfect defence:

> It is the duty of every person who has care of a child under 16 years to— (a) provide the necessaries of life for the child; and (b) take the precautions that are reasonable in all the circumstances to avoid danger to the child's life, health or safety; and (c) take the action that is reasonable in all the circumstances to remove the child from any such danger... [s286(2) includes a "person who has care of a child" includes a parent, foster parent, step parent, guardian or other adult...]

If the defendants had not acted as they did, they would have broken this law. But the court wants to exclude the child abuse from being heard by the jury. The CDPP successfully applied to the court to have s286 excluded from the trial. Judge Clare specifically stated (justifying the exclusion) "Whether the children were abused or not is not relevant." The judge has also excluded s70NAE(4) of the *Family Law Act 1975* as a defence; that Family Court orders may be breached with reasonable excuse such as to protect a child from harm. This defence enlivens s10.5 Lawful authority. *Criminal Code Act 1995* (Cth)... A person is not criminally responsible for an offence if the conduct constituting the offence is justified or excused by or under a law...

Some readers might be familiar with YouTube vlogger Shaun Attwood. For several years he was one of the main sources for exposing Jeffery Epstein and Ghislaine Maxwell. In a video (18 September 2023) he explains that those who stand up against the 'power structure' would have their reputations destroyed, and could land up in prison. He says,

"The legal system is a tool of these people. They snap their fingers and these things get done. I was exposing the co-conspirators of Jeffrey [Epstein] and they snapped their fingers. The next thing I was in a London police station getting threatened with prison and had to agree to a caution. The cop opposite me said this has come from up top."

This is how it works. Anyone challenging the status quo (i.e., exposing child abuse or unlawful removals) is punished by the regime. And it's a regime that protects child abusers. Why did John Howard suppress 28 high profile names for 90 years? Every official or judicial officer involved in Operation Noetic court conspiracy case has some knowledge of the child abuse disclosures in the evidence. They confiscated Russell and Patrick's computers that contained the evidence. Surely, they are legally obligated to act on any suspicions or risks, but astonishingly no one ever asks about the children – and whether they are safe in the care of the people they reported as their abusers. An astounding dereliction of their legal duties!

Instead, the CDPP Crown prosecutors are hiding the exculpatory evidence, and the court seems intent to impede, in every possible way, the truth from getting out; or that a police officer blatantly lied about the child abuses. When Patrick wanted to expose "the credibility of the [police] officer", Judge Clare replied, "This is not a trial of the police officer... you are the one on trial" (or wording close to that).

It's like government and court officials are operating on a specific thought-frequency, where their minds cannot access what is morally the right thing to do (for children). Many protective parents have described the courts as instruments of black magic. God help us when truth is concealed and the protectors of children are punished.

It feels like this case is a barometer of the moral compass of Australia.

As an addendum to this chapter, I will discuss the "33-Minute Murder Case."

I was approached a few years ago by a producer friend who suggested we do a movie on Said Morgan. I had not known about the case, but include it as it demonstrates the public's standards and expectations of protecting children.

Said Morgan was a detective in NSW, and in May 1995 had something to do with charging his brother-in-law, Mansour Suha, with sexually molesting three young girls, two being Said's nieces. On being granted bail, Suha laughed at Said and intimated that his nieces would not live to testify. Said went to Suha's Oakhurst home, flashed his detective's badge at the woman who answered the door, walked passed a teenage boy, and found Suha in bed. In an action described in court as a "Clint Eastwood notion of justice", Said emptied his service revolver, shooting the man six times. Dead!

Said called the Fairfield Police Station telling his colleague that he's just shot Suha; and refused an offer by his colleague to plant a pistol. He went to trial and faced charges of murder; and despite the judge's instructions that they must bring in a guilty verdict, the jury took just 33 minutes to decide his actions were justified.

Public debate erupted, with thousands supporting his actions; with one 8-year-old boy writing: *"Dear policeman, I'm glad you shot a child molester. I know how bad they are and what they do."*

It seems society's values (e.g., a jury) are in conflict with the values of the courts. Today in plain sight, authorities continue to fail society and have become the protectors of sexual abuse perpetrators. The world has turned upside down; the government is intent on hunting down and prosecuting those who attempted to protect children from sexual abuse.

Floppy Arms & Fractured Families

This chapter is about two infants with floppy arms.

Any parent will understand that a baby dominates a parent's existence. For the first few years of their life you are constantly feeding them, protecting them, or nurturing them. Several months ago, in the same week, two cases (from separate states) arrived in my Inbox. (I've now heard of many more almost identical cases.) In both cases, the first-time parents, from a place of concern and caution, decided to take their baby to hospital because of a 'floppy arm'. There seemed little wrong with the babies on arrival at hospital – and both sets of parents were trying to do the right thing, and get their infants checked on, just to be sure.

In the one case, the young first time dad was walking with his dog on the beach, with his baby in his arms. A large dog started to threaten his small dog, and still holding his baby he tried to intervene and pick up his dog. Later that afternoon the parents noticed a floppy arm and decided to get it checked at the hospital. A fracture was found and the hospital alerted the child protection department.

The baby was removed, and the father charged by the police with Assault causing Bodily Harm. The police used severe tactics to harass the parents, searching their home, removing their phones and installing phone taps, in an attempt to make the dad plead guilty. He consistently refused as he had no idea how the baby had been injured accidentally. He's been required to stand trial in the Criminal Court and during this period his punitive bail conditions gave him minimal access to his child and partner, including no photos or videos. (One hour before publication, I received an email; "The prosecution in Perth have dropped the case.")

This means the family has effectively missed out on the all-important first year of life. The mother has likewise been denied access to the child, despite not being charged, because she allowed

167

the dad to walk with the baby, and enabled the "assault" by the father. Despite the baby's arm being entirely healed in 2 weeks, the infant is still under the Guardianship of the department (in Western Australia). The couple is considering having another child. But the department has told them that even if the father is found Not Guilty, they will not relinquish guardianship of this child or any subsequent children. This one incident could therefore result in a life sentence for the couple regardless of the Court's decision.

In the other case, the young mum took her newborn to hospital over a concern of a floppy arm. On arrival at emergency, her baby was calm and there was no bruising or swelling on the arm. Her baby was whisked off to the doctor – and that's when her and her partner's world imploded. This is what she wrote in an email:

> "...I took him in with a floppy arm, and I was absolutely shocked to hear there was a fracture... I was immediately separated from him and interrogated in a room by a man, with no support. I didn't have a clue what was going on at the time. When I returned from this interrogation room, I was shown a photo on a computer screen of a broken arm. I suspected and questioned from the beginning - what happened in that X-ray room or in the time when I was separated from my son. We were admitted overnight to the [redacted] Hospital and DOCS/Police arrived the following morning and began their interrogations. Police were much easier to deal with... and it was extremely intense and distressing from the beginning. In the second X-ray at [redacted] Hospital, after the transfer, I witnessed them contort his little body over and over. And I had NEVER heard him scream like that. He wasn't crying when I noticed his arm, or when I was checking it, or when I took him to the car, or in the car, or as I carried him into the hospital ER. After this second X-ray, I was then told he had multiple fractures and given the Temporary Assessment Order. The final set of X-rays, taken after he was taken into

custody of the department; they came back with a cartoon diagram of a child's body (no scans) and we were told there were multiple fractures…"

One has to ask what *the* doctor did when putting the infant through "contortions." Were any fractures worsened?

The parents pleaded with the doctors, including the so-called independent second opinion doctor, to do a thorough and deeper medical investigation. The doctors deliberately did not do this in the beginning -- when time was crucial to discover any relevant medical evidence and data. TBBD (Temporary Brittle Bone Disease) was just one of the conditions they asked about. The medicos refused to even investigate for the most commonly found cause, Osteogenesis Imperfecta, until their lawyer threatened to go to the Supreme Court. Finally, the doctors reluctantly agreed to do genetic screening for conditions that cause brittle bones. After the parents subpoenaed the medical records, the hospital that had allegedly conducted the genetic testing said that there were no records of their son, X. Did the hospital lie to parents about the testing being done? Or was something found in this test and now it's conveniently gone "missing"?

The department submitted multiple 300+ page Affidavits to Court against the parents – presenting the alleged "evidence." However, I am told, these documents from start to finish are full of lies, mistruths and exaggerations -- as I would have expected! In another case, in a department psychologist's 30-page report there was a factual error or a blatant lie in every single paragraph.

What is extraordinary and extremely concerning is that the department (Department of Child Safety), the Hospital and the Right to Information Department all refused to produce any of X's medical records. The parents eventually had to apply to the court and subpoena their own child's medical records.

Why, and what might the medico's or hospital be hiding?

In the WA case, the X-ray given to the police was nothing like the X-ray done on arrival at the hospital and sighted by the mother. They too were not given access to their baby's medical records.

It appears there is a DEFAULT position that the parents are to be blamed first — before anything.

There is also information that one specific doctor is tied to a number of these almost identical infant-removal cases — and that she is acting in a rogue manner. There should be an inquiry into this QLD doctor (and others) regarding medical malpractice and her falsifying notes. I have recently been alerted to many other couples losing their baby after presenting at a hospital. The *modus operandi* is the same: the child (so-called) protection paediatricians immediately accuse the parents of abuse. The medicos' then set about the task of backing up their claim with false information or by conveniently failing to do a thorough medical investigation. Consider: if there is misconduct going on in multiple hospitals (and several medicos) for just one case, what does the mean for all the other cases so similar to this family's case? From the patterns emerging, it seems clear that certain medical professionals are facilitating these removals -- yet they are untrained to assess a forensic or psychological investigation outside their expertise with regard to child neglect or abuse.

These parents were trying to care for their infants, wanting reassurance by getting them checked -- but it seems a doctor 'targeted' them. We pray these parents get their babies back, and I am hoping that the social workers in these instances identify the love and dedication of these parents and try correcting the matter. I have to also consider the possibility of some "benefit" for a doctor to take this position. Is this 'harvesting' (gathering) of infants, sourced from hospitals across the country, somehow orchestrated from above? The big question: we know a baby is worth millions (as asset of 18 years to the OOHC service industry), so how many infants are wrongfully removed annually?

A Plea from a Mother

I was cc'd into this email to the two good doctors [names redacted] to help offer medical solutions.

Dear Dr P and Dr K,

This is the compassionate plea for help from a desperate mother, driven to extreme levels of exhaustion... My mother, who has kinship care, has nearly suffered a stroke yesterday after the Department have relentlessly traumatized her, and she is currently in hospital and unable to care for her grandson at this time. My newborn baby has been taken to a Foster Care home 1.5 hours away... I pleaded with the Department to be allowed to deliver breast milk (which I previously did) but the response was that the Foster Carer was not going to facilitate the delivery of breast milk. My son has been denied his human right to breast milk and has been taken away from my family without any information provided as to what was happening to him. It is an unbearable thought to know my little baby is somewhere completely unfamiliar, with no one that he knows, no comforts that he knows at all.

I would never harm my child, nor would my partner, and we don't know how he has broken bones but we believe that it highly likely happened at birth due to a fast dystocia birth. I do agree with Graeme [Bell], there has to be a plausible explanation why my baby has [x] fractures. However, Ray has spoken to a legal aid lawyer that had a previous life as a doctor; and no judicial officer will accept anything but the parents, or someone to have caused these injuries unless there is medical evidence of an alternative narrative.

Please, if you can help me, I will be forever grateful.

Kind regards, [mother of N]

A Prayer from a Father

I, along with Pastor Paul and others received this email (extract):

...It's taking me a while to compose myself to write this message as I couldn't hold back my tears, when my heart is overwhelmed with love and gratitude I just want to start by saying that I cannot find the words to truly express my gratitude I feel towards you for helping my beautiful partner and I with all the advice, support and love in this fight for my beloved son. When my darling delivered him into this world he became everything, my soul is tethered to him, I would trade my life for his without hesitation or thought. When he was taken from us, two loving parents who planned his birth right up to the moment of conception, my world shattered into pieces, I can't even begin to comprehend how his Mother feels. If it wasn't for my absolute weapon of a Fiancé, who, with all your help, works tirelessly day and night without stopping, I don't know if I would have had the capacity to survive this brutal and heartless attack alone. I naively assumed that because of our innocence, that the justice system and the department, along with our cooperation and voluntary invitation into our lives, would assess that X is clearly in no danger and would be swiftly returned, I have never been so wrong.

What has happen to our beautiful Nation... My heart and soul aches for all the families, mothers, fathers and children that are facing similar circumstances. We truly are in a battle against principalities and the rulers of darkness, and wickedness and high places, I keep you all in my heart when I pray... This is an absolute injustice beyond this world and I pray for these wicked, Godless people, one day they will have to face their maker.

...My darlings, oh my heart aches for my beautiful babies, God help them...

God Bless / Loving Father, Partner and Friend

A Pastor's Fight in a Perfect Storm

Very few people on this earth are prepared to dedicate their lives to people they don't know. Even fewer are prepared to give (even give up) their lives to save children. This not only requires courage, selflessness and empathy, but a powerful moral belief and love for humanity.

One of the loudest and boldest voices is Pastor Paul Robert Burton, and so I had asked him to write the Foreword of this book. He covered many topics and it was like jumping into the deep end. I decided to split his writing, and place this part in this section "Prosecuting Protectors." Not only is he a protector being prosecuted, but once the reader has a clearer grasp of the 'industry' his writing will hopefully resonate more deeply with the reader. The rest of the chapter is by Pastor Paul:

"Over six years ago now, shortly before I met Dee, myself and around eight other members of our community were pepper sprayed and assaulted trying to prevent a four year old highly compromised indigenous child being forcibly ripped by two Family and Community Service caseworkers, and around 32 armed police, in Newcastle NSW. This shocking event was fortuitously live-cast and went viral on social media reaching around 500,000 people within minutes and around 4 million people in a matter of hours.

The Department of Family and Community Services (FACS) formerly DOCS and now called The Department of Communities and Justice (DCJ), had removed this child on known FALSE grounds. And yes, they certainly provide a 'service' alright, a forced and violent removal service, operating without delegated authority, and removing children with no judicial oversight, often based on false and misleading information. It took around two years challenging FACS with multiple cases in multiple jurisdictions, in these (alleged) courts, to finally reunify him with his parents,

173

notwithstanding of course that the damage of these forced and often violent removals is largely irreversible.

Families rarely if ever fully recover.

Oh, and it would be remiss of me not to mention that I have now officially been suppressed with a continued regime of interlocutory injunctions by the Supreme Court of Equity NSW since June 2017. And as a consequence of what was originally 10 criminal charges (7 that are still yet to get to trial in 2024 or 2025) for allegedly saying a child's name on Facebook. I have appeared before more magistrates and judges than any other self-represented individual in Australia fighting this draconian system that will stop at nothing to persecute its victims and protect the government, and the associated criminal perpetrators of child trafficking and child abuse.

These governmental organisations literally abduct children for profit and then go running with the screaming children under their arms into these CLOSED secret children's courts (that are not courts by any stretch of the imagination) where the magistrates rubber stamp the removals and ensure they continue a "gravy train" of near seamless destruction of poor hapless families for significant profits. The children are then deprived near all contact with their biological families and "shunted off" into an independent, largely unmonitored, privatised, exponentially expanding Out Of Home Care (OOHC) system.

According to the productivity commission this is now around an 8½ billion dollar national industry and growing at an alarming rate. And, dare I say, the sicker a child is the more they are worth, again according to the productivity commission. The annual cost per child in care as of the 30th June 2021 varied across jurisdictions ranging between $60,408 and $128,918. Annual costs were considerably higher for residential care ranging between $455,480 and $881,113 compared to non-residential care ranging between $41,358 and $54,460. And most regrettably this is only the tip of this enormous financial iceberg.

So of course, when a child is removed, that child becomes traumatized, when the child is traumatized and kept from his or her family, the trauma increases, as the trauma increases so does the child's financial value. The parents also suffer the same fate, for as their trauma also increases they too end up, depending on how they respond, either entering into the health system (that I would rather call an 'illth' system, largely because of the negative impacts of these child removals on their spiritual and mental health), or they end up (because of their struggles and inability to process the anger at the injustice that has befallen them) in the now fully privatized prison system.

It's a strange kind of "chicken and egg thing". The Department claim they take children because the parents may for example have mental health, drug and anger management issues, however the parents inevitably often develop those mental health, drug and anger management issues because the Department has taken their children. Then following this they are effectively "gas lighted" in these "star chamber" style secret closed children's courts, denied near all contact with their children. The trauma this induces needs to be witnessed to be believed. Spouting things to the parents like "If you don't do all the parenting courses and jump through all of our hoops you will never see your children again." And even if they do jump through all those hoops most parents rarely ever have their children returned because quite simply, there is no money in that, the money is in the removals.

It's the "Perfect Storm." The OOHC system profits (using of course the National Disability Insurance Scheme), the medical professionals profit, the courts profit, the lawyers profit, the court appointed psychologists profit, the jails profit, the police profit and of course the government profits as the multi-national corporations providing these products and services work with them to ensure the legislation protects them all from being exposed.

Oh yes, and let's not forget the near fully controlled media that profits through their paid silence and 'vomitous' propaganda.

"Another child stolen by someone known to them" - you mean the parents have tried to get back their own child!

"King Pins of an international child trafficking syndicate" – oh, you mean a mother and grandmother were helped by a few good people because they were trying to protect their children that had disclosed sexual abuse!

"An anti-medicine cult leader, head of QAnon and part of an international extremist military religious order" ... Oh that's me Pastor Paul, I'm truly honoured!

I recall the words of Yeshua Ben Josef in Matthew 23

> *"13. But woe unto you, scribes and Pharisees, hypocrites! for ye shut up the kingdom of heaven against men: for ye neither go in yourselves, neither suffer ye them that are entering to go in."*

> *"14 Woe unto you, scribes and Pharisees, hypocrites! for ye devour widows' houses, and for a pretence make long prayer: therefore ye shall receive the greater damnation."*

> *"23. Woe unto you, scribes and Pharisees, hypocrites! for ye pay tithe of mint and anise and cummin, and have omitted the weightier matters of the law, judgment, mercy, and faith: these ought ye to have done, and not to leave the other undone."*

Massive profits for ALL in the system at the expense of these poor hapless families and their children.

I often wonder what kind of world we would have if people, rather than selfishly making billions of dollars through the mechanisms of greed, fear, division, anger, hatred and shocking intergenerational trauma created by supporting this appalling industry that profits from the often irreversible abuse of our children, if we instead applied the higher principles of the "philosophia perennis" and heeded the timeless words of The Beatles and John Lennon with "All You Need Is Love" or "Imagine".

Just imagine a world where these same energies and huge financial resources were used to truly assist the thousands and thousands of traumatised families and children; a world where Peace, Love, Compassion, Truth and Real Justice prevails."

"Atmano mokshartham jagat hitaya cha" For One's own welfare and the welfare of all. - *Swami Vivekananda*

"Speak out on behalf of the voiceless, and for the rights of all who are vulnerable." - Prov 31:8

"There is nothing concealed that will not be disclosed, or hidden that will not be made known" - Luke 12:2

"Not by power nor by might, but by spirit sayeth The Lord" - Book of Zechariah 4:6

Amen

Pastor Paul Robert Burton

Pastor Paul Robert Burton (Minister of Religion, Bard, Environmentalist, Paralegal and Human Rights Advocate.) www.pastorpaul.com.au

"If you ask me the one thing I know for sure; 200,000 pieces of data, I know that in the absence of love and belonging there's always suffering. -- *Brené Brown*

My Closing Statement – 'Wheel of Misfortune'

I believe the system is past redemption – not because it is a failed system, but because it was DESIGNED to do what it does.

How do you fix a three-century-long culture of 'stealing' children? The toxic mindset of 'removals' amongst many public servants, executives, ministers and commissioners is so deeply entrenched that it has become 'standard-issue' for them – i.e., it has been NORMALIZED. It has become common practice to punish the child (by removing him or her) when a parent is suspected or accused of something that cannot be demonstrated or even proven. It's reclamation of the *Court of Oyer and Terminer* of 1692 -- the present-day version of the Salem Witch trials.

Apologies for any repetition in this final summation, but how can one consider it in the best interests of a child when three officers forcibly grapple a desperate screaming girl or boy from the person they love deeply (mother and/or father) and then subject that child to the extreme form of psychological abuse of separation for the remaining of their child and teen years? The same displaced and vacuous destiny awaits a breast feeding baby when it is ripped from its mother's breast on shaky or spurious claims.

Is this a sign of a mentally ill and deeply sick society?

There is one disparity that's worth a mention. When sexual abuse by a child is reported, it is generally ignored or concealed by agencies, and the court reverts to disbelief. However, if there is an injury or medical issue with an infant, the protocol is to *automatically* blame the parents for abuse. These are not rationally consistent – but both have the same outcome: i.e., removing (trafficking) the child from the protecting parent or parents.

It's also a crime to emotionally abuse or psychologically harm a child. To quote FACS (NSW)[66], "Serious psychological harm can occur where the behaviour of their parent or caregiver damages the confidence and self-esteem of the child or young person, resulting in serious emotional disturbance or psychological trauma." It's beautifully put, but in so many cases when the government becomes the parent (guardian), it is the department that CAUSES the harm and psychological trauma.

The government is a proven bad parent.

The removed child is also initially left in limbo-land. When parents challenge the department in court, how can it be deemed in the best interests of a child when it can take more than two years of protracted court processes to facilitate an outcome (especially when the child desperately wants to go home)? Again, is this a DELIBERATE delay tactic? I have also lost count the number of times I have heard this mantra, "Your Honour, the child has been in her placement for two years now, and has settled well with the foster family. Placing her back with her parents would be disruptive for the child at this time." Case settled!

The default thinking is to remove children from the frying pan into the fire. However, it is known and accepted that children in OOHC or foster care are in more danger of being raped and abused, and more likely to have social challenges and face poorer life-long health outcomes. Children are over 20X more likely to die whilst in care. Why would a court, charged with a child's safety, have a default position to place the child and at greater risk (in State care)? And we have no idea of how many of these children were taken from happy nurturing homes. (Some of those parents might have needed some assistance, and again, I am not referring to those children who need and/or want to be rescued.)

Unlike the distraught parents in publicized kidnappings on the news, if the department takes your child, you have to be compliant, subservient, and accepting that they are doing what's right. Really! And if you publicize that your or someone else's child has been taken, you'll be breaking their 'keep it all secret' laws — and punished (like Pastor Paul and Dr Katelaris). A tiger mother will kill to save her cubs, but when mothers and fathers follow their natural human instincts to fight for their children, the department looks down on this. When challenged, the department will most likely bring out the big guns and amass the resources of government to crush you. And if you protect a child from further sexual abuse (as a result of an erroneous family court order) they will hunt you down (like they've done to Dr Pridgeon and O'Dea). I often wonder why government has turned on its own people.

I posed the question in the Prologue whether human rights and the law apply to children – and whether they have been unjustly "deprived of their liberty"? I believe tens of thousands of children over the last few decades have been deprived of their liberty.

I, and others like Pastor Paul, have in the past suggested that an axe murderer would get more contact with their children than a parent who has lost a child to the system -- like Joanne and many others (there are hundreds of Joanne's in Australia). When I was to direct some episodes of Wentworth (the television series) some years back, I was taken to the women's prison outside Melbourne. I met with and spoke to some women 'crims'; even met two incarcerated mums who had their young children in with them. A murderer has more legal standing in a criminal court than a parent being subjected to a department's whims and fancies in the Children's Star Chambers. The facts around a murder are dealt with in every detail – beyond doubt. However, an opinion or a trumped-up illusory accusation is enough to send a child and parent on a hideous journey of parental apartheid.

I remind you that Joanne still has lawful sole custody (an order of the federal Family Court), yet she was (and is) NOT allowed phone calls, no messaging or social media contact with her daughter, no school attendances at plays or sports day, or be present at family get-togethers (if her daughter is there). No words can express my disgust at how people can think this is acceptable, and why some members of the family just go along with this folly. (How easy is it for authority to realign compliance in the brain?)

And PJ has had NO contact with her son for 6 months now, with the department planning to keep mother and son apart until he turns 18. I have yet to see any 'reasonable' claim against her. In a judgement to appoint a litigation guardian, the claim against PJ is "…that [she] has chronic fixed paranoid ideas about government corruption and stealing children. [She] was discharged on Olanzapine [a drug for schizophrenia]." Hang on a moment, should those million or more anti-government protestors in the last few years also lose their children and be forcibly medicated? This is the most extreme form of THOUGHT CRIME… and punishment -- and they can only get away with this 1984-style denunciation because it's SECRET.

So back to the jury-convicted murderer v the (non-convicted) Star Chamber protective parent (e.g., Joanne, PJ). So, let's "compare the pair" (as per the Industry Super ad). The protective mum might have one hour supervised visitation every fortnight with all other contact forbidden (or no contact). Meanwhile the 'crim' will have his or her relationship with their child 'protected' by the prison system. There was a NSW Parliamentary Inquiry, "Support for Children of Imprisoned Parents in New South Wales," and "It is generally understood that visits to see incarcerated family members are good for children, families and those in prison." This is what is published on the South Australian 'Corrections' site[67]:

> "Visits can help the child and the parent deal with the pain of being separated. Along with helping to maintain their relationship … Parents in prison are able to make a telephone call… Regular short conversations with young children may be more satisfying than a longer one… It's helpful for children to hear their parent's voice, even for a short time… Letters are a fantastic way for children to maintain contact with a prisoner." [These actions are encouraged]

The criminal has more legal standing than a protective parent. And the child has NO legal protections at all.

I repeat: The criminal has more legal standing than a protective parent, and the child has NO legal protections at all.

The child and parent caught up in the child or infant removals racketeering business are dealt a brutal blow. The law, the country and its leaders have completely abandoned them. Everything is done to keep them apart – and no expense (of misappropriated funds) is spared to do so. And no outsider is privy to the secret machinations of the Star Chambers when the spider's web slowly cocoons them. "You cannot disclose anything about the case … this is for the privacy and protection of your child." "But, Your Honour, if the malfeasance of this case is made known… made public, this will then protect my child from a life of psychological harm and separation."

The secrecy laws are principally there to protect the actions of wrongdoers.

In 1877 they did not attempt to hide the fact that Mary Ann Langley had been raped by her father when a young teen. And at least journalists wrote about it, back then. In the 1877 article, the author opined: "the law should be amended as soon as it can be done, in order that criminals like him [Charles] may not escape without rigorous punishment, so that such revolting practices maybe rooted out from amongst us." There are laws now, but no one is following them. In 2019, I was communicating with *The Age* for over four months. I flew Joanne up to Melbourne for a meeting – and we were stood down; they got cold feet. I wrote to the editor and sub-editors asking why; they said a South Australian story would be of no interest in Victoria. I offered three Victorian stories but no …they're not game to expose State child trafficking, and should revert to printing their news on yellow paper.

Children's court is like a twisted game -- a Wheel of Misfortune!

Many of the magistrates and judges in these Star Chambers 'washing' children through the children's courts seem to be unaware, or just ignore, the disastrous consequences to society their orders cause. Furthermore, these devastating outcomes are shrouded in secrecy and go unchecked as most parents, worn-down by the abusive, gas lighting process, are unable to challenge.

I've read some convoluted judgments, and despite the seemingly convincing verbiage, they lack rational thought, reasonableness, and social perception. They regularly violate the Rights of the Child and punish protective parents with a sentence of parental isolation and destitution without any basis in fact. What happened to innocent unless proven guilty? In the end, the outward appearance is that the children's court magistrates and judges are mere 'deputies' of the child departments. And the Australian child protection industry is following the same narrative and *modus operandi* as the criminal global child protection empires as described by Nancy Schaefer.

This is more than *schadenfreude*, it's a booming business designed to profit off the resource: CHILDREN. It's a 'jobs and growth' profit-driven service industry in disguise that ruptures Australian society. It should end, but how do you change a cultural locked-in perceptual thinking in the political arena? However, if the 'protection racket' was made public; if stories were made public, every single agency and organization involved would at least be put on notice. Politicians would have to listen.

I've said before, there are children that need to be rescued, and there are some good people in the system doing just that. I'm sure many public servants would like to operate in a more ethical and transparent way – and not through the trafficking Star Chambers. The other day, my medical friend told me about his sister; she's a psychologist and went into child protection, but she lasted only a few months. She was so distraught she left for New Zealand and sought a change of career in hospitality.

I've reflected on how the court treated Ella for four years. I imagine this happens to THOUSANDS of other children and infants, and so I advocate for the closure of the Children and

Youth courts; they do not operate as courts of law, nor do they follow the law as it was originally intended. They harm children. At least open the courts and provide open justice for the child.

And to those ICLs (Independent Children's Lawyers) that seem to have no idea of what children are about, what they dream for or how their minds work -- must depart that profession. Imagine not even consulting your 'client' on a forever life-changing decision. More thought and care is given to a stray dog at the RSPCA (and this makes me feel physically ill thinking about it). No one has more power over someone's destiny. They must be aware of the tricks of the department, and I'm sure this exchange, as exampled below, has been repeated in many courts across the country:

ICL addresses the court, "The report says the child, after 5 months, is now settled into her new school, and has found new friends, Your Honour." Magistrate, "Is there visitation for her to see her parents?"

Barrister for the department (the Crown), "That has been reduced to one hour a month now, Your Honour. At the end of supervised visitation the child was becoming acutely distressed, and it was determined the parents were encouraging this behavior by giving hope to the child that they'd get her home."

The mother cries out from the back, "They told us we are not to tell her we love her---" Magistrate, "QUIET... your solicitor will speak for you." The legal aid lawyer looks back at them nervously, whispering, "Don't upset the court."

The Crown barrister continues, "The department has found a placement in a town 80 kilometers away, Your Honour, as they felt the child's familiar surrounds had an adverse impact on her, and feared her school friends' parents might disobey orders and allow unsupervised contact with the defendants."

The father holds his sobbing wife. Parent's Lawyer, "Your Honour, the parents want me to remind the court that their child wants to come home." Magistrate, "I got that, thank you. And…" The magistrate turns to the ICL. ICL, "I support the department's view, Your Honour… that, that the child remain under guardianship until the age of 18."

Magistrate, "Have you met with the child?"

ICL, "Err… No, Your Honour."

This is how cruelty is NORMALISED.

And to those psychologists and psychiatrists who prostitute the codes of their profession, and act so faithlessly against children in their well-compensated reports – you are the ones that are mentally ill, and you should be subjected to psychological and ethics testing. Many should be struck from their profession.

And for all those public servants who act unlawfully (e.g., concealing evidence, altering statements, blatant lies, etc.) and knowingly place children in harm's way, you should face inquiries, prosecution, and the full force of the law. (One has to ask why company directors are going to jail for work and safety offences (accidents) when child protection workers are being protected.) A 'red flag' should be put against the names of those who have done wrong, and they should be forbidden to have a 'Working with Children' card for as long as they live. They are the racketeers.

In Joanne's case, ALL these persons and the court disregarded the law, abandoned every human right of the child, and then knowingly, maliciously, and deliberately cooperated (conspired?) with each other to firstly, abduct the child from her mother; secondly, attempt to place her (via Reunification court) with the person she'd claimed (for 4 years) had abused and raped her (thankfully Ella resisted and saved herself); then, thirdly remove her permanently from her mum because she bravely spoke out. She did not know the word rape, nor understand the criminal and legal severity of the actions done to her, but it's clear she understood that she had been violated. (*Re-read this paragraph.*)

Beware! All these people are in charge of other children? They are in charge of thousands of children.

Don't tell me that justice exists in this penal country. Many suggest this is a spiritual war between good v demonic forces? The dark days are now, and we can lead you to many people surviving in this living hell. Are these racketeers in alignment with society's values, or has this country lost its way? The system is wrecking the sacred parent-child bond, eroding the foundation of love, and the miracle of our human existence.

Would a Royal Commission be sufficient? I don't believe so. I don't see a way to overhaul the system. We need to stop profiteering off children, put an end to the present 'child protection racket' and create a new way. In my humble opinion, every single executive and supervisor in the present system should be removed and have to reapply. Many of these people should never work with children again. This will create a space to attract new and better people. Police forces should be strained of officers that act against children (there are plenty of good officers), and the Ministers of child protection (past and present) should be stood down and subject to inquiry. What was their participation?

I believe it would be easy to *start* correcting the matter if there was a will. Secrecy laws could easily change (as per Pastor Paul's s105 court challenges) to protect children and NOT the department or any sexual perpetrator. You can follow every ship or plane – live – across the world, so why is the placement of a precious child held in such secrecy? Is it so the parent can never make contact or the child can't contact his or her parent; or is it to secure the acquired "merchandise" from being reclaimed or found? (If there was no wrongful removal, there'd be no reason for dire secrecy.) I believe there is no way for an outsider or estranged family member to locate a child in the system. Why? *Please tell me if there is.*

An audit of removals in every court and government agency with the names of case workers, police officers, psychologist, plus the OOHC agency involved over the last 20 years could be assimilated into a (public) data base (children could be identified as initials and numbers). AI systems could quickly analyze the patterns of potential exploitation of those department offices, public servants and agencies involved. Advertising nationally for people to call in and submit their accounts could initiate an honest and open process to review unwarranted and unlawful removals outside of the department-controlled children's courts.

An independent authority like a People's Commission could deal with unlawful or unwarranted removals applications and direct a specialist unit to identify the crimes of public servants to be dealt with in a criminal court. It will take decades to reinvent the 'protection' system, but these organizations could be set up to work alongside the present child protection agencies; to hold the present corrupted system to account. They would be the only real 'check and balance' structure available. They may be initially overwhelmed with thousands of cases, but it would be a start, and they would undoubtedly return children to deserving parents. And any costs associated with funding these new bodies could be from redirected budget savings of having fewer children in OOHC.

I believe Canberra would be most reluctant to expose this racket and downgrade a lucrative service industry, especially if there's a possibility of massive compensation payouts. We hope our politicians have the stomach to listen and face this reality. As I wrote in the beginning, I hold this book out to you – like a lit candle to shine a light on humanity. For those leaders and influencers in Australia that are reading this, please do not blow this candle out; rather use it as a blow torch to help change our world for the better.

We need to get to grips with reality: that the so-called child protection system is nothing but a "PROTECTION RACKET."

Postscript

In this book, I have not expanded on the "exploitation" of children once they have been drawn away from their families (as indicated in the diagram on p84) as that deserves its own book.

We know that orphanages and institutions in the 1950s and 60s, for example, were a source of fodder for pedophiles. Teens were collected from these institutions and taken home on week-ends, not to experience the outside world, but to be used. We have heard about sex trafficking, child sacrifices, demonic rituals, organ harvesting, and Adrenochrome production. We can only pray that most children in State guardianship are spared this exploitation.

I often think that this is humanity's scripted dark journey on this earth. The sacrifice, in all its forms, of children has gone on for millennia. I had thought that humans had elevated to a higher more ethical frequency, but it seems not. Personally, the battle within me is to quell my rage, to find compassion for all, and try forgiving those who act with such disregard and maliciousness... for "they know not what they do." But I resent doing the child ministers' job; it has sent me broke, whilst they're earning hundreds of thousands annually, to further benefit from bloated pensions. They should be listening to these parents who desperately seek help – but they operate on an "out of sight, out of mind" strategy. Sadly, they probably know exactly what's going on, and their hearts and souls may have been extorted or enslaved to cooperate in this toxic, demonic or destructive frequency.

There's the implication in the title that this is all about racketeering – about making money, but I believe financial reward is just the bonus, just the oil greasing the engine. All the Western countries operate their child protection industries in a similar way, and there's a global congruency – of patterns – that reflect, I believe, a much larger and darker agenda. It's like an unseen entity harvesting the magical energy of the innocent, and feeding off their trauma. I am not sure of the ultimate purpose, but we know that the all the systems – big pharma, agriculture, food production, media, education, etc., are designed to manipulate our perception; to disrupt our immune systems and our natural ways. The WEF mantra is "You'll own [or have] nothing and you'll be happy…" And that will include your children.

Richard Day, MD., in his 1969 lecture at the Pittsburgh Pediatric Society, described how the 'controllers' have long-planned the destruction of the family. He said "Everything is in place, nothing can stop us now."[68] So much of what he described then has come to pass since his lecture over 50 years ago: from wars, weather, food control, scientific research, sex, terrorism, finance, new diseases, surveillance and the arrival of global totalitarianism.

Is humanity being prepared for a new dark future? Facing a potential upgrade (or down grade)? Many aspects of society are leading *Homo sapiens* towards a chaotic Trans-human agenda and Post-human future. It took only a few years to cast biology aside; now there are 100 genders for children to choose from. Parental rights have been drastically downgraded; mothers are no longer treasured -- but they've become birthing agents. And you are encouraged to think that your children belong to the collective. Governments across the world have taken more and more control over you and your children's lives and their perception of reality.

Children are the key – and the Child Removals Racket is perfectly in line with this dehumanizing agenda and playing its part in the grand societal destruction. The disruption of children's lives results in the disintegration of the integral and miraculous aspects of parenting, comprehending love, and being human.

This agenda, whatever its ultimate purpose, is ANTI-HUMAN.

Thanks

This book started from a casual conversation one afternoon a few months ago with Russell (Dr Russell Pridgeon) when we were discussing the predicament of children in Australia. Russell simply concluded, "Dee you just *have* to write a book." I was further inspired by my good friend Kyls who intimated that this was the 'time' mapped out in my life-path (she then inspired the title).

But I want to thank the many, many people who have supported, educated and inspired me along this journey; from Pastor Paul, Mary Maxwell, Graeme Bell (for being my legal tutor), Darren Dicksen (constitutionwatch.com.au), Rachel Vaughan, Russell, Patrick, Ange, Lana, Marney, Kieran (Dr), Andrew K (Dr), Renae, Eugenia Patru (USA), Diane dV, Bevan J, Serene T, Ray, Yolande Lucire, George P, Charles, Emma, Mishka, Lisa, Mel, Ann, Elspeth, Gabbi, Brae, Deb, Roland, Claudia, Pat, the Bowdens and many other amazing people; and to the mothers, fathers, foster parents, and grandparents, who so bravely live and fight to tell their stories. Those names I can't reveal and anyway I would not want to leave someone out. I also thank the supporters of Gumshoe News and those generous people who have made donations to assist me with this work.

To those people in the system trying to do good, keep doing what you do for children. We want to support you to expose the corruption and make things better.

To those thousands of children who suffer under this regime, we pray for you to be strong. Please be strong; refuse to be a victim, and make every effort to free yourself. This book was written for you all.

"Kids weren't believed back in the 60s and 70s" --
Lawrence Hall, abuse survivor (The Age 30/11/2023)

(Sadly children are still not listened to in 2023...)

It's a crime to conceal a crime.

A person may be considered an accessory after the fact when they have helped with the destruction or concealment of evidence that may implicate an offender (e.g., the child sexual offender); or given false information with a view to diverting their investigations away from the offender.

Some Statistics

These Child Protection statistics (Australia 2019–20) are sourced directly (and unaltered) from aihw.gov.au.[69]

During 2019-20, 174,700 (31 per 1,000) Australian children received child protection services (investigation, care and protection order and/or were in out-of-home care). Aboriginal and Torres Strait Islander children were 8 times as likely as non-Indigenous children to have received child protection services. Children from geographically remote areas were more likely to be the subject of +substantiation, or be in out-of-home care than those from major cities. Over 5,300 children were reunified with family during 2019–20

Summary:

Each year, around 3% of all children aged 0–17 are assisted by Australia's child protection systems. Some children are unable to live safely at home as they may be at risk of being abused or neglected, or their parents may be unable to provide adequate care. Children and their families may receive support services to keep children with their families, or be subject to investigations of reports of child abuse/neglect, protection orders, and/or placement in out-of-home care, such as with a relative or foster carer.

This report presents statistics on state and territory child protection and family support services, and selected characteristics of children receiving these services. This includes statistics for 2019–20, and trends over the 5-year period from 2015–16 to 2019–20.

1 in 32 children aged 0–17 received child protection services in 2019–20

174,700 children received child protection services in 2019–20.

More than half (57%) of these children were the subject of an investigation only, and were not subsequently placed on a care and protection order or in out-of-home care. A small proportion of children (7%) were involved in all 3 components of the system.

67% of children receiving child protection services were repeat clients—that is, the children had previously been involved with the child protection system.

Emotional abuse was the most common type of abuse or neglect

Emotional abuse (54%) was the most common type of abuse or neglect substantiated through investigations in 2019–20. This was followed by neglect (22%), physical abuse (14%), and sexual abuse (9%). A higher proportion of girls (13%) were subject to sexual abuse than boys (6%), while boys had slightly higher percentages of substantiations for neglect and physical abuse.

Children from remote areas had the highest rates of substantiation

Children from *Very remote* areas had the highest rates of substantiation (24 per 1,000 children) and were more than 3 times as likely as children from *Major cities* (7 per 1,000 children) to be the subject of a substantiation in 2019–20.

Almost 46,000 children were in out-of-home care

At 30 June 2020, of the approximately 46,000 children in out-of-home care, 92% were in home-based care. Most of the children in out-of-home care (94%) were on care and protection orders and 67% had been continuously in out-of-home care for 2 years or more.

Trends over time for children in out-of-home care

The number of children in out-of-home care rose by 7% between 30 June 2017 and 30 June 2020 (from 43,100 to 46,000). During this time the rate of children in out-of-home was relatively steady at 8 per 1,000 children.

Trends for children in out-of-home care have been affected by varying definitions over time. From 2018-19, all jurisdictions report out-of-home care data according to a national definition and time series analyses in this report have been back cast to 2016–17. Out-of-home care data in this report should not be compared with data published prior to *Child protection Australia 2018–19*.

Over 30,600 children had been in out-of-home care for 2 years or more

At 30 June 2020, of the approximately 30,600 children in long-term (2 years or more) out-of-home care, 82% were on long-term guardianship orders and in either relative/kinship care (11,200) or foster care (11,300).

Of the children in long-term out-of-home care, 2 in 5 (42%) were Indigenous.

Almost 6,700 children exited out-of-home care to a permanency outcome

Of the 6,700 children exiting to a permanency outcome during 2019–20, around 5,300 were reunified with family (19% of children in out-of-home care for whom reunification was a possibility), 1,200 were placed in a third party parental care arrangement (2% of children in out-of-home care) and 162 were adopted (less than 1% of children in out-of-home care).

1 in 6 Aboriginal and Torres Strait Islander children received child protection services

Indigenous children continue to be over-represented among children receiving child protection services, including for substantiated child abuse and neglect, children on care and protection orders and children in out-of-home care.

In 2019–20, 55,300 Indigenous children received child protection services, a rate of 166 per 1,000 Indigenous children—an increase from 151 per 1,000 in 2016–17.

14,300 Indigenous children were the subject of substantiation in 2019–20. The most common type of substantiated abuse for Indigenous children was emotional abuse (47%) followed by neglect (32%).

At 30 June 2020, 23,300 Indigenous children were on care and protection orders. Of these children, 68% (15,900) were on guardianship or custody orders.

1 in 18 Indigenous children (around 18,900) were in out-of-home care at 30 June 2020, almost two-thirds (63%) of whom were living with relatives, kin or other Indigenous caregivers.

Over 4 in 5 Indigenous children (84%) who exited out-of-home care to a permanency outcome in 2018–19 did not return to care within 12 months.

Index

End Notes

[1] https://humanrights.gov.au/our-work/commission-general/international-covenant-civil-and-political-rights-human-rights-your

[2] https://humanrights.gov.au/our-work/commission-general/universal-declaration-human-rights-human-rights-your-fingertips-human

[3] https://www.aihw.gov.au/reports/child-protection/child-protection-australia-2020-21/contents/out-of-home-care/how-many-children-were-in-out-of-home-care

[4] https://www.smh.com.au/entertainment/books/the-story-of-the-wretched-boys-who-were-transported-to-australia-20190830-p52mew.html

[5] https://m.facebook.com/nt/screen/?params=%7B%22note_id%22%3A366895537763248%7D&path=%2Fnotes%2Fnote%2F&refsrc=deprecated

[6] https://www.afp.gov.au/news-centre/media-release/stop-human-trafficking-happening-plain-sight

[7] https://www.vic.gov.au/stolen-generations-reparations-steering-committee-report/chapter-2-victorian-stolen-generations-0

[8] https://www.creativespirits.info/aboriginalculture/politics/stolen-generations/stolen-generations-stories#uncle-robert-paul-youngs-story

[9] https://www.google.com/search?q=dhhs&oq=dhhs&aqs=chrome..69i57j0i512l3j0i131i433i512l2j0i67i433i650j69i60.1055j0j7&sourceid=chrome&ie=UTF-8

[10] https://www.facs.nsw.gov.au/resources/publications/annual-reports

[11] https://josephinecashman.substack.com/p/i-uncovered-a-child-trafficking-and

[12] https://josephinecashman.com.au/protecting-children

[13] https://www.facs.nsw.gov.au/resources/publications/annual-reports

[14] https://www.facebook.com/paulrobertburton

[15] https://www.aihw.gov.au/reports/child-protection/child-protection-system-in-australia

[16] https://kangaroocourtofaustralia.com/

[17] https://www.unicef.org.au/united-nations-convention-on-the-rights-

of-the-child

[18] https://www.washingtonpost.com/national/health-science/what-separation-from-parents-does-to-children-the-effect-is-catastrophic/2018/06/18/c00c30ec-732c-11e8-805c-4b67019fcfe4_story.html
[19] https://www.facebook.com/watch/?v=10155550659937196
[20] https://www.judiciary.uk/wp-content/uploads/JCO/Documents/Judgments/j-a-child-judgment.pdf
[21] https://historycollection.com/the-cruelest-human-experimentation-cases-in-history/
[22] https://historycollection.com/the-cruelest-human-experimentation-cases-in-history/
[23] https://gumshoenews.com/ministers-for-child-protection-lose-their-immunity-in-six-australian-states/
[24] https://www.psychologytoday.com/us/blog/the-couch/201010/how-do-you-explain-human-cruelty
[25] https://gumshoenews.com/action-part-4-legislatures-can-lift-a-courts-technical-roadblocks-to-justice/
[26] www.dss.gov.au/sites/default/files/documents/12_2021/dess5016-national-framework-protecting-childrenaccessible.pdf
[27] https://www.facs.nsw.gov.au/resources/publications/annual-reports
[28] *Stoltengorgh, van Ijzendoorn, Euser, & Bakersman- Kranenburg,* 2011
[29] *Hunter,* 2011; *Jonzon & Lindblad,* 2004; *Ullman,* 2007
[30] https://www.alecomm.com/index.php/50-governments/australia/nsw/nsw-ombudsman/649-children-in-out-of-home-care-in-nsw-are-twenty-five-times-more-likely-to-die-than-children-living-at-home-with-parents
[31] https://gumshoenews.com/statistical-evidence-gumshoes-family-court-survey/
[32] Collin-Vézina, De La Sablonnière-Griffin, Palmer & Milne, 2015 p.123,
[33] https://www.alecomm.com/index.php/50-governments/australia/nsw/nsw-ombudsman/649-children-in-out-of-home-care-in-nsw-are-twenty-five-times-more-likely-to-die-than-children-living-at-home-with-parents
[34] https://www.theage.com.au/politics/victoria/serious-shortfalls-in-victoria-s-working-with-children-checks-ombudsman-20220913-p5bhkv.html

35 https://www.afp.gov.au/what-we-do/crime-types/fraud/fraud-and-anti-corruption

36 https://www.afp.gov.au/what-we-do/crime-types/human-trafficking

37 http://www5.austlii.edu.au/au/legis/cth/consol_act/ca191482/s42.html

38 https://www.counterfraud.gov.au/explore-fraud-problem

39 https://www.afp.gov.au/what-we-do/crime-types/fraud/fraud-and-anti-corruption

40 https://www.afp.gov.au/what-we-do/crime-types/human-trafficking

41 https://www.dol.gov/agencies/ilab/our-work/child-forced-labor-trafficking/child-labor-cocoa

42 Bureau of International Labor Affairs estimates 1.56 million children are engaged in hazardous work on cocoa farms in Côte d'Ivoire and Ghana.

43 https://gumshoenews.com/wp-content/uploads/2023/11/productivity-commission.png

44 https://www.aihw.gov.au/news-media/media-releases/2021-1/may/rate-of-children-in-out-of-home-care-remains-stabl#:~:text=The%20report%2C%20Child%20protection%20Australia,of%2Dhome%20care%20across%20Australia.

45 https://www.aihw.gov.au/reports/australias-welfare/welfare-workforce

46 https://www.abc.net.au/news/2021-12-09/family-matters-report-indigenous-children-removed-from-homes/100685932

47 https://data.unicef.org/topic/child-protection/children-alternative-care/

48 https://brokensystemproductions.com/shared-parenting-paradigm/

49 https://theconversation.com/factcheck-how-much-of-australias-tax-is-collected-by-states-and-territories-50457

50 https://www.abc.net.au/listen/programs/backgroundbriefing/6651696

51 https://www.aihw.gov.au/reports/children-youth/australias-children/contents/justice-and-safety/child-abuse-and-neglect

52 https://gumshoenews.com/the-pedophile-racket-part-2-emotional-abuse-and-trashing-a-good-mum/

53 https://www.abc.net.au/listen/programs/backgroundbriefing/6651696

54 https://www.ranzcp.org/getmedia/2e090981-cdd2-4dee-a317-f8718bc7dc47/ranzcp-code-of-ethics.pdf

55 https://breggin.com/Psychiatry-as-an-Instrument-of-Social-and-Political-Control

56 https://gumshoenews.com/foster-children-of-the-state-the-garbage-bag-children/

57 https://gumshoenews.com/unimaginable-and-hidden-cruelty-by-child-protection-departments-and-courts/

58 https://gumshoenews.com/statistical-evidence-gumshoes-family-court-survey/

59
https://www.youtube.com/watch?v=13jindxNw28&t=2s&ab_channel=WILTY%3FNope%21

60 https://gumshoenews.com/its-time-the-institution-of-the-law-face-reality/

61
https://m.facebook.com/nt/screen/?params=%7B%22note_id%22%3A366895537763248%7D&path=%2Fnotes%2Fnote%2F&refsrc=deprecated

62 https://parentalrights.org/wp-content/uploads/2017/05/CBCP.pdf

63 https://www.winterwatch.net/2022/09/was-nancy-schaefer-assassinated/

64
https://www.youtube.com/watch?v=twnLK5uMz4o&ab_channel=YvetteBronx

65
https://www.youtube.com/watch?v=k1CTpgwk5LE&ab_channel=GumshoeNews

66 https://www.facs.nsw.gov.au/families/Protecting-kids/reporting-child-at-risk/harm-and-neglect

67 https://www.corrections.sa.gov.au/family-and-friends/children-with-a-parent-in-prison

68 https://gumshoenews.com/everything-is-in-place-and-nobody-can-stop-us-now-dr-day-1969-lecture/

69 https://www.aihw.gov.au/reports/child-protection/child-protection-australia-2019-20/summary

Printed in Great Britain
by Amazon

43168786R00115